1 BUSINESS VENTURE

WORKBOOK

Roger Barnard & Jeff Cady

Angela Buckingham

OXFORD
UNIVERSITY PRESS

Great Clarendon Street, Oxford OX2 6DP

Oxford University Press is a department of the University of Oxford.
It furthers the University's objective of excellence in research, scholarship,
and education by publishing worldwide in

Oxford New York

Auckland Cape Town Dar es Salaam Hong Kong Karachi
Kuala Lumpur Madrid Melbourne Mexico City Nairobi
New Delhi Shanghai Taipei Toronto

With offices in

Argentina Austria Brazil Chile Czech Republic France Greece
Guatemala Hungary Italy Japan Poland Portugal Singapore
South Korea Switzerland Thailand Turkey Ukraine Vietnam

OXFORD and OXFORD ENGLISH are registered trade marks of
Oxford University Press in the UK and in certain other countries

© Oxford University Press 2009

The moral rights of the author have been asserted

Database right Oxford University Press (maker)

First published 2009
2014 2013 2012 2011 2010
10 9 8 7 6 5 4 3 2

ISBN: 978 0 19 457802 8

Printed in China

ACKNOWLEDGEMENTS

Sources: p 12 information from www.sony.net, www.hyundai.co.uk, www.
jollibee.com.ph, www.evergreen-marine.com; p 38 information from www.
lauraashley.com

Cover image courtesy of: Getty/Justin Guariglia.

*We would also like to thank the following for permission to reproduce the following
photographs*: Alamy Images pp 31 (forklift/vario images GmbH & Co.KG), 38
(Laura Ashley shop/Maurice Savage), 51 (Diner/Jeff Greenberg), 57 (Hong Kong
market/JLImages), 57 (Long tailed macaques/Leonid Serebrennikov), 67 (Email/
INSADCO Photography); Corbis pp 4 (meeting/Randy Faris/Flirt), 14 (reception/
Dennis Cooper/zefa), 25 (businesswoman/Gerhard Steiner/zefa), 57 (Kowloon
Jade Market/Kelly-Mooney Photography); Getty Images pp 6 (Long set table/
Omer Knaz), 9 (presentation/Christoph Wilhelm/Photographer's Choice), 19
(Indie band the Red Riders), 23 (Woman on golf course/Jetta Productions), 37
(assembly workers/Forrest Anderson//Time & Life Pictures), 66 (businessmen/
Steve Edson Photography/Photonica); OUP pp 10 (Portrait of Businessman/
Photodisc), 23 (Customer Services Representative/Photodisc), 23 (Architect/
Photodisc), 49 (basketball/Corbis), 55 (man reading map/Image Source), 66
(Singapore skyline/Photodisc), 67 (Mobile phone/D.Hurst); Photolibrary pp 4
(Three executives walking/Dex Image), 23 (Graphic artist/Corbis), 23 (Woman
shopping for shoes/Polka Dot Images), 43 (sushi bar/Dominic Dibbs/Fresh
Food Images), 57 (Peak Tram sign/Cade Martin/Uppercut Images), 67 (Handing
out businesscards/VStock), 67 (City map of New York/ImageShop/Corbis);
PunchStock pp 20 (Businessman in office/Image Source), 23 (Businesswoman
holding graph/Blend Images).

Illustrations by: Peter Bull pp 21, 16, 55, 56, 69; Javier Joaquin/The Organisation
p 8; Simon Williams/Illustration p 35.

Contents

First meetings

MODULE 1.1

Complete the conversation. Use the words below.

meet   trip   pleased   start   this   welcome

A *Good morning. Come in. I'm Jun Nakamura.*
B *Lewis Baker. _____ [1] to meet you.*
A *Pleased to _____ [2] you too. _____ [3] to Nagoya.*
B *Thank you.*
A *Did you have a good _____ [4] here?*
B *Pretty good, thanks.*
A *Let me introduce you. _____ [5] is Ms. Motegi, our Sales Manager.*
B *Hello.*
A *Would you like some coffee before we _____ [6]?*
B *Yes, please. Thanks.*

Talking about yourself

1 Look at the information about these four people. Answer the questions.

Example
Where is Ms. Griffin from?
She's from Melbourne.

	Heather Griffin	**Yeong-Min Han**	**Ruby Cheng**	**Kentaro Abe**
From	Melbourne	Seoul	Hong Kong	Sapporo
Lives	Singapore	London	New York	Kuala Lumpur
Company	Apple	Hyundai	Ikea	Sony
Job	sales manager	engineer	accountant	marketing manager

a   Where is Mr. Han from?

_____

b   Who does Ms. Griffin work for?

_____

c   Where does Ms. Cheng live?

_____

d   What does Mr. Abe do?

_____

Look at the information again. Write the questions.

e   _____

She's from Hong Kong.

f   _____

He works for Hyundai.

g   _____

He lives in Kuala Lumpur.

h   _____

She's a sales manager.

2 Now write about yourself. If you can, add some extra information.

_____

_____

_____

Numbers 1–10; telephone numbers

1 Look at the flight information. Answer the questions.

Flight no	Destination	Time	Status
BA 179	**New York**	0815	Gate closed
VS 201	**Sydney**	0825	Boarding Gate 17
CX 251	**Hong Kong**	0845	Boarding Gate 35

Example
What time does the flight to Sydney leave?
It leaves at 0825.

a Which flight goes to Sydney?

_____

b What time does the flight to New York leave?

_____

c Which flight is boarding from gate 35?

_____

d Which gate do you need for flight VS 201?

_____

2 Look at the information. Write the questions.

Useful telephone numbers:

Narita Airport
0476-34-8000

Japan Railways
050-2016-1603

a _____?
It's 0476-34-8000.

b _____?
It's 050-2016-1603.

c _____?
My cell number? It's 0236 789 1432.

MODULE 1.4

1   Read the information on these business cards.

2   Match the names on the left with the correct information on the right.
   a   Studio Software Design   is a teacher of engineering.
   b   Miho Ishida   is on the twelfth floor.
   c   Mark Wilson   has offices in Taipei.
   d   Bryce Anderson   is a book company.
   e   Dr. Wu   works in the Sales Department.
   f   Yoshiro Takeo's office   is an accountant.
   g   Kangnam International   is a software designer.
   h   Michael Tseng   has branches in Tokyo, Seoul,
                                         London, Singapore, and Hong Kong.

MODULE 1.5

Look at the business cards in Module 1.4 again. Complete the sentences.

a Yoshiro Takeo works in _____.

b Dr. Grace Wu _____ for the University of Chattanooga in Tennessee.

c You can contact Michael Tseng by mail, e-mail, or _____.

d The Web Design Services office is in _____.

e The _____ for Bryce Anderson Financial Services is Sanden Building, 22nd Floor, 5-5, Kojimachi 4-Chome, Chiyoda-Ku, Tokyo 106.

f You can contact Go Yong Sun by _____. His address is sungy@ kangnam.co.kr.

g Dr. Wu's telephone number is (1) 615 9123 146. Her _____ number is 1472.

MODULE 1.6 Culture file – Greetings

Look at the pictures and read the diary page. Fill in the missing words.

arrived   bowed   exchanged   met   shook   went

Monday
I _____ at Narita Airport, Tokyo on Saturday. Mr. Takeda _____ me at the airport. We _____ business cards and _____ hands. We _____ by limousine bus to the hotel in Tokyo city center. The hotel staff _____ when they showed me to my room.

2 You and your company

MODULE 2.1 Introducing your company

1   These people are talking about their jobs. Fill in the blanks in the dialogue. Use the words below.

department   pleased   for   organize   with   in   do

A *Let me introduce myself. I'm Jan Cheung.*
B *_____¹ to meet you, Ms. Cheung. My name's Michael Barton.*
A *Which company do you work _____² , Mr. Barton?*
B *I'm _____³ IBM. I work at the headquarters. I'm _____⁴ the market research _____⁵.*
A *I see.*
B *How about you? What _____⁶ you do?*
A *I'm a training manager with Samsung. I _____⁷ training for our sales representatives.*
B *Oh, that's interesting.*

2   Read the conversation again and look at the information below. Answer the questions.

IBM manufactures and sells computer hardware and software.
Samsung makes consumer electronics (telephones, MP3 players, etc.).

a   Who does Mr Barton work for?

_____

b   What does the company sell?

_____

c   Where does Mr. Barton work?

_____

d   Who does Ms Cheung work for?

_____

e   What does the company make?

_____

f   What does she do?

_____

MODULE 2.2

1   Complete the sentences about the companies. Use the words below.

Example
Kookmin Bank
Kookmin Bank is a *Korean company. It provides banking services.*

~~Korean~~   American   Australian   Chinese
Japanese   American   Japanese

~~provides banking services~~   provides banking services   sells fast food
provides telecom services   makes cars
sells food products   makes electronic business products

a   Toyota

_____

b   China Mobile

_____

c   Kraft

_____

d   Ricoh

_____

e   National Australia Bank

_____

f   KFC

_____

2   Ken Lee describes his job. Read what he says.

"My name is Ken Lee. I'm a marketing manager with J.T. Lennox, an advertising agency. I organize market research and produce promotional material. We have clients in fourteen countries.

Now write about your job. If you can, add some extra information.

_____

_____

_____

MODULE 2.3

1 Complete the table.

Job		Activity	
1	administrator	administrate	
2	_____	design	
	developer	3	_____
4	_____	manage	
	organizer	5	_____
6	_____	supply	

2 Match the job with the department and activity. Complete the sentences.

Example

I'm an accountant. I work in the Finance department. I manage the staff payroll.

Job	Department	Activity
~~accountant~~	Human Resources	check customer orders
website manager	~~Finance~~	organize staff training
training manager	IT	~~manage the staff payroll~~
sales representative	Customer Service	manage the company website
office clerk	Sales	demonstrate new products

1 I'm a _____

2 I'm a _____

3 I'm a _____

4 I'm an _____

MODULE 2.4

1 Match the numbers to the words.

12	thirty	16	eighteen
20	fifteen	60	ninety
13	twelve	17	sixteen
30	forty	70	seventy
14	fifty	18	eighty
40	thirteen	80	sixty
15	twenty	19	seventeen
50	fourteen	90	nineteen

2 Read the information about some of Asia's major companies.

> ### Sony
>
> Sony has more than 163,000 employees and over 50 factories worldwide. The 63-year-old Japanese company is involved in music, movies, and consumer electronics.

> ### Hyundai Motor Company
>
> Hyundai is the world's 5th largest car maker. The South Korean car company has its headquarters in Seoul. It manufactures cars worldwide, including in the US, China, and Europe. It produces about 4 million cars a year.

> ### Jollibee
>
> The Jollibee Food Corporation is the top fast food chain in the Philippines. It has more than 50 restaurants in over 5 countries. It has branches in the United States, Vietnam, and Hong Kong.

> ### Evergreen Marine Corporation
>
> One of the world's largest shipping companies, EMC covers more than 80 countries with its shipping network. It has more than 150 ships and is based in Taipei.

Write the questions using the information above.

Example
How many employees does Sony have?
More than one hundred and sixty-three thousand.

a How many _____?
   Over fifty worldwide.

b How many _____?
   About four million per year.

c How many _____?
   More than 50 stores.

d How many _____?
   More than one hundred and fifty.

MODULE 2.5

Starting a conversation

Complete the conversation.

A *Ms. Shaw? My _____¹ Gloria Cheng. I really enjoyed your presentation.*
B *Thank you. Where do you _____², Ms. Cheng?*
A *I work _____³ Yahoo, in Hong Kong.*
B *Oh, really?*
A *Yes, I'm in the Customer Services _____⁴.*
B *And what do you _____⁵?*
A *I'm a sales executive.*

1   Read the e-mail and answer the questions.

✉ **E-mail**

From: Lorenzo, George [lorenzog@arpproductions.com]
To: Ms. Grace Wu
Subject: My visit to Beijing

Dear Ms. Wu,
Thank you for your offer to meet me at the airport. My flight number is CA 452. That's Air China. It arrives at 2:30 p.m. on November 4th.

I look forward to meeting you then.

Best wishes,
George Lorenzo

a   Who is the e-mail from?

_____

b   Who is it to?

_____

c   What is it about?

_____

d   What is George Lorenzo's flight number?

_____

e   What time does his flight arrive?

_____

2   Write a similar message to Ms. Wu. You are going on a business trip to Shanghai. Use the information below.

flight to	Shanghai
airline	Japan Airlines
flight number	JL 765
your arrival time	6:00 p.m.
date of flight	December 12th

✉ **E-mail**

From: _____
To: _____
Subject: _____

_____
_____
_____
_____
_____
_____

3

Visiting a client

MODULE 3.1

Arriving for an appointment

1 Complete the phrases. Use the words below.

how   meet   take   this   you

a _____ are you?

b Please _____ a seat.

c I'd like _____ to meet Mr. Abe.

d _____ is Ms. Yasuda from Apple.

e Pleased to _____ you.

2 Number the conversation in the correct order.

Oh, I'd like you to meet our Marketing Manager. This is Kenji Ito. ☐

Come in, Mr. Lewis. It's very nice to see you again. How are you? ☐ 1

Hello, Mr. Ito. It's good to meet you. ☐

I'm fine, thanks. ☐

Please, take a seat. Would you like some coffee before we start? ☐

Yes, thank you. ☐

Good to meet you, too, Mr Lewis. ☐

MODULE 3.2

At reception

Look at this list of appointments at Mitsubishi's Hong Kong office. Write what each visitor says. You are the last visitor.

Example
10:30 / John Golden / Hideo Nakanishi / NKK
Good morning. I have an appointment with Mr. Golden at 10:30.
I'm Hideo Nakanishi from NKK.

a   11:15 / to see Teruo Kawasaki / Grace Ma / Ricoh

_____

b   2:20 / to see Marilyn Held / Toshi Ikeda / Futura Computers

_____

c   3:00 / to see Younha Lee / Richard Bolton / Asia Week magazine

_____

d   3:30 / to see Frank Allen / you / your company or college

_____

MODULE 3.3

Meeting people

Read these jumbled conversations. One is formal and one is informal. Write them into the correct box below.

Hey, Pon-chan.

Good morning, Mr. Park.

Hi, Jake. How's it going?

Good morning, Ms. Green. How are you?

Not so bad. How are your folks?

I'm very well, thank you.

Please have a seat. Would you like a cup of coffee?

Pretty good, thanks.

Have a seat. Tea? Coffee?

Thank you. Coffee would be nice.

Coffee, please. Thanks!

FORMAL	**INFORMAL**

Finding the right room

These people are at the information desk at the international auto expo. Look at the floor plan and fill in the blanks. Use the words and phrases below.

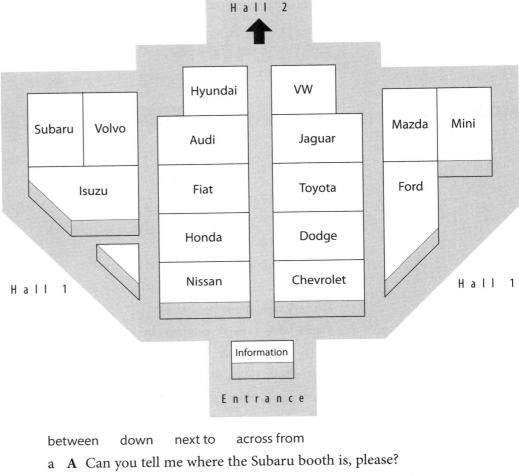

between   down   next to   across from

a **A** Can you tell me where the Subaru booth is, please?

  B Yes, it's over there, _____ the Volvo booth.

b **A** Could you tell me where the Hyundai booth is?

  B It's down there, _____ the VW booth.

c **A** Excuse me, where's the Fiat booth?

  B It's _____ there on the left, just past the Honda booth.

d **A** Excuse me, I'm looking for the Jaguar booth.

  B Certainly, it's down there on the right, _____ the Toyota booth and the VW booth.

MODULE 3.5

Numbers 100–10 000, addresses

1 Match the numbers to the words.

100	one thousand	120	twelve thousand
1000	ten thousand	1200	one hundred twenty
10000	one hundred	12000	one thousand two hundred

2 Write these numbers in words.

a 250 _____

b 3000 _____

c 970 _____

d 180 _____

3 Write your address (or your work address) in English.

4 Look at this envelope. Match the parts of the envelope (a–c) with the descriptions below.

a Avalon Farms, Inc.
400 Dry Creek Rd.
Avalon, IA 50707 USA

b **CONFIDENTIAL**

c **Mr. F. MacManus**
Marketing Manager
Fitzgibbons and Brown
5678 Main St.
Halifax, Nova Scotia
B3J 2NJ
Canada

the address of the person you are writing to (the addressee) ☐

the return address (writer's address) ☐

the mailing information ☐

5 Number the address information in the correct order for an address in the US.

a street address ☐

b state ☐

c company ☐

d ZIP (postal) code ☐

e person's name ☐ 1

f country (for international mail) ☐

g his / her position in the company (optional) ☐ 2

h town or city ☐

6 Match the mailing information phrases (a–d) with the definitions (1–4).

a CONFIDENTIAL 　　1 It will break easily.

b FRAGILE 　　2 It should be sent as quickly as possible.

c DO NOT BEND 　　3 Only the addressee should read it.

d URGENT 　　4 Keep it flat.

7 You work for Banner Creative Arts Company. Your company address is:

463 Whitebrook Drive West, San Francisco, CA 94110.

Address two envelopes to your overseas clients. Use one of the mailing information phrases in Exercise 6.

a You are sending some important photographs to Henri Leclerc in Paris. He is the Personnel Director. His address is: Accents S.A., 18 Rue de Tocqueville, 75430 Paris.

b You are sending a contract for Jordi Pros to sign. He is the Marketing Manager. His address is Fotosina S.A., Fortuna Building, 4th floor, 21 Calle Roig, 08005 Barcelona.

MODULE 3.6

Culture file – What's your office like?

1 Read the text.

The Portable Office

Gerard Mercier is a management consultant with Neilson Consulting. Mercier doesn't go to the office every day. Like most of Neilson Consulting's staff, he spends 80 percent of his time with clients. When he needs to work at the company's head office in Paris, he phones to reserve a place in a 'virtual office'. When he arrives, there is a desk with a telephone and plugs for his laptop ready for him. His file cabinet on wheels has been moved from a store room to his 'desk for the day'. Mercier loves the new system. 'We meet different people, and it's very cost-effective. We save a million dollars a year in rental costs.'

2 Are these statements true or false? Check (✓) the correct box.

		True	False
a	Gerard Mercier works for a management consulting company.	☐	☐
b	He spends 80 percent of his time at his office.	☐	☐
c	The company's head office is in Paris.	☐	☐
d	He can reserve a place at the head office by phone.	☐	☐
e	Each desk has a computer.	☐	☐
f	His file cabinet always stays in the same place.	☐	☐
g	Mercier likes working in a 'virtual office'.	☐	☐
h	The company spends less on rent because of the new system.	☐	☐

Business activities

MODULE 4.1 Describing routines

1 Bill Edwards is a personnel manager with a transportation company. Match the questions (a–f) with the answers (1–6).
   a What do you usually do when you arrive at the office?
   b When do you attend meetings?
   c Where do you have lunch?
   d What do you do after lunch?
   e Do you work overtime?
   f How often do you go out with your colleagues after work?

   1 Usually in the morning. The managers get together once a week.
   2 We have a drink in a local bar about once a month.
   3 Yes, I usually work at least one extra hour a day.
   4 I sometimes go to the cafeteria, but I often go out for lunch.
   5 I always check my e-mail first.
   6 I usually do deskwork in the afternoon.

   a ___   b ___   c ___
   d ___   e ___   f ___

2 Now answer the same questions about yourself. You can use true or imaginary information. Write your answers below.

   a _____
   b _____
   c _____
   d _____
   e _____
   f _____

1   Read this article about being successful in business.

John Banner is the CEO of a manufacturing company. He has a simple approach to work – he never mixes his job with his private life. 'I always arrive home thinking about my family and not my work. When I get to work in the morning I usually feel really refreshed and ready for another day.'

'Never be satisfied' and 'Always question things' are his two rules. 'I often have an idea because I'm not happy with the way something works.' Another good example of this is James Dyson, the inventor of the Dyson vacuum cleaner, who wasn't happy with the way his old vacuum cleaner worked. 'People like Dyson are always thinking about how things can work better,' says John. His other business guru is Steve Jobs, the CEO at Apple Inc. 'Steve is like me. He knows that he sometimes makes mistakes, but he doesn't worry. He just gets on with the job.' Another similarity is that John doesn't always ask the customer what they want. 'They always say they want A, and when you make A they say they want B. Focus groups occasionally give you the right answer. But usually you should use your own judgment and talk to designers, the people who are creative and see into the future.'

2   Answer the questions about John Banner.

a   What does he think about his job and private life?

He never _____

b   What is he thinking about when he gets home?

He is always _____

c   What are his two rules?

'Never _____' and 'Always _____'

d   When does he often have an idea?

He often has an idea _____

e   What do people like James Dyson always think about?

They always think about _____

f   Do focus groups always give you the right answer?

No, they _____

MODULE 4.3 — Talking about company activities

1 Sara Berry's Ice Cream Company is producing some new flavors of ice cream. Read the stages. Number them in the correct order.

- ☐ the customers buy the product
- ☐ introduce the new flavors
- ☐ 1 do market research
- ☐ organize advertising campaigns
- ☐ run trial tests for the flavors
- ☐ get product endorsement

2 Now write a paragraph about this process. Use *first / next / then / after that / finally.*

At Sara Berry's, we take great care when launching a new flavor of ice cream
onto the market. First, we do market research.

_____

_____

_____

_____

_____

_____

MODULE 4.4 — Numbers and times

1 Write the times in words.

nine ten   1 _____ 2 _____ 3 _____ 4 _____ 5 _____

2 Write the times in words.

a quarter   1 _____ 2 _____ 3 _____ 4 _____ 5 _____ 6 _____
after two

3 Look at the flight departure board below and answer the questions.

Flight	Carrier	Destination	Departure
QF 3445	Qantas Airways	Dusseldorf	9:05 AM
AC 869	Air Canada	Toronto	9:09 AM
VS 3	Virgin Atlantic Airways	New York	10:08 AM
MS 9231	Egyptair	Cairo	11:10 AM
IB 7443	Iberia	Madrid	11:18 AM

a Which flight goes to Toronto?

_____

b What time is the flight to New York?

_____

c Where does flight number QF 3445 fly to?

_____

d What time is the flight to Cairo?

_____

e What time is the flight to Madrid?

_____

4 Write about your typical day. Answer the questions.

a What time do you usually get up?

_____

b What time do you usually arrive at work?

_____

c What time do you usually have lunch?

_____

d What time do you usually arrive home?

_____

1 Look at the information about these people and their jobs. Match two of the phrases below with each person. The first one has been done for you.

1 Grace Bennett
financial analyst
[d] [k]

2 Ted Finlay
freelance illustrator
[ ] [ ]

3 Anna Babic
store manager
[ ] [ ]

4 Derek Chan
sales representative
[ ] [ ]

5 Ayako Yamamoto
pro golfer
[ ] [ ]

6 Jack Givens
architect
[ ] [ ]

a   always works in his studio at home
b   sells office equipment
c   occasionally does work for Time magazine
d   ~~works for a securities company in New York~~
e   works for a large construction company
f   sometimes travels long distances to visit customers
g   usually plays in the United States
h   sometimes designs new office buildings
i   works for a shoe store chain
j   sometimes appears in TV commercials
k   ~~often visits companies to get information~~
l   manages the Fifth Avenue branch

2 Choose two of the people above. Write about them like this:

Example
Grace Bennett is a financial analyst. She works for a securities company in New York. She often visits companies to get information.

1 _____

_____

_____

2 _____

_____

_____

3 Write three or four sentences about your job, or a job you would like to do.

_____
_____
_____
_____

MODULE 4.6   Business writing – e-mail

1 Read these e-mails.

> ✉ **E-mail**
>
> Dear Mr. Burton
>
> The design for the new office is now ready, and I would like to show it to you. Would 3:00 p.m. on Monday, October 21st at your office be convenient?
>
> Best wishes
> Jiro Nakamura

> ✉ **E-mail**
>
> Dear Mr. Nakamura
>
> Thank you for your e-mail about the design for the new office. 3:00 p.m. on Monday, October 21st at my office is fine.
>
> I look forward to seeing you then.
>
> Best wishes
> Jeff Burton

2 You received this e-mail today. Write a similar reply.

> ✉ **E-mail**
>
> Dear (your name)
>
> The market research figures are now ready, and I would like to show them to you. Would 10:00 a.m. on Wednesday, November 12th at your office be convenient for you?
>
> Best wishes
> Betty Wang

> ✉ **E-mail**
>
> Dear _____
>
> _____
> _____
> _____

Fixing an appointment

MODULE 5.1 | Arranging to meet

1 Look at Carla Wade's schedule for the week. Write the questions.

Diary			
Monday	**Tuesday**	**Wednesday**	**Thursday**
10:30 meeting Carolyn Black to discuss e-commerce	9:45 meeting Ken Park to discuss website design 12:30 meeting Marc Alder for lunch	10:00 meeting Miho Harada to discuss sales conference	

a What's _____ ?
   She's meeting Carolyn Black to discuss e-commerce.

b What's _____ ?
   She's meeting Ken Park.

c Is _____ 11:30?
   No, she isn't. She's meeting him at 12:30.

d When's _____ ?
   At 10:00 on Wednesday.

2 What are your plans for this week? Write three sentences.
Example
On Friday at 3:00 I'm meeting Mr. Abe to discuss the sales figures.

a _____

b _____

c _____

MODULE 5.2

1 Read this memo.

> *a.m.*   *Call George Hansen (Toyota Motors, Marketing Dept)*

Complete the telephone conversation. Use the words below.

could   one   this   do   morning   speaking

A *Good _____¹ Toyota Motors. How may I help you?*
B *Yes, _____² I speak to Mr Kato in Marketing, please?*
A *_____³ moment, please. I'll put you through now.*
C *Hello, George Hansen _____⁴.*
B *Hello, Mr Hansen. _____⁵ is Junko Kato from Bridgestone.*
C *Hello, Ms Kato. What can I _____⁶ for you?*

2 Write the name, company, and department of a person you want to call in your diary below. Then write a similar conversation.

> *p.m.*   *Call _____ (_____ , _____)*
>   (name)   (company)   (dept.)

A _____
B _____
A _____
C _____
B _____
C _____

MODULE 5.3

1 Akira Sato calls Julia Weber to make an appointment. Number the lines of the telephone conversation in the correct order.

B *How about here on Thursday morning at 11:00?*   ☐
B *Hello, Julia. It's Akira Sato here.*   ☐2
A *Great. I'll see you then. Bye.*   ☐
A *Next week would be fine. When do you have in mind?*   ☐
A *Julia Weber speaking.*   ☐1
B *Bye.*   ☐
B *2:00 p.m. on Thursday would be fine.*   ☐
A *Hi, Akira. What can I do for you?*   ☐
B *Could we meet next week to discuss the budgets?*   ☐
A *I'm sorry, but I'm busy all morning. But how about the afternoon, say 2:00 p.m.?*   ☐

2 Now write a similar conversation. Use the following information.

Paula Kellerman calls Eiji Takahashi. She wants to meet this week to discuss sales targets. She suggests Friday at 3:00 p.m., but Eiji is busy all afternoon. He suggests 10:30 a.m., and they agree to meet then.

A _____
B _____
A _____
B _____
A _____
B _____
A _____
B _____
A _____
B _____

MODULE 5.4

Numbers – ordinal numbers; dates

1 Unscramble the words to find all twelve months of the year. Then write the calendar order (*1st, 2nd, 3rd … 12th*) next to the correct month.

Example

runyjaa	*January*	*1st*
tugusa	_____	_____
ootberc	_____	_____
yam	_____	_____
deeebrcm	_____	_____
befyruar	_____	_____
yulj	_____	_____
mepstbeer	_____	_____
unej	_____	_____
breeovmn	_____	_____
plira	_____	_____
charm	_____	_____

2 Write the dates below as they are spoken.

Example
month / day / year
1 / 2 / 06
January second, two thousand and six.

a 3 / 10 / 84

_____

b 5 / 15 / 01

_____

c 7 / 28 / 08

_____

d 9 / 30 / 04

_____

e 11 / 1 / 10

_____

3 Answer the questions.

1 What is today's date?

_____

2 When is your birthday?

_____

3 When did you start your job at this company?

_____

4 When does your vacation begin this year?

_____

1 Read the conversation. Then answer the questions.

Jeff Baker	*Could we meet sometime next week to discuss the new project?*
Pete Smith	*Of course. When do you have in mind?*
Jeff Baker	*How about Tuesday afternoon?*
Pete Smith	*I'm sorry, I'm busy. I have meetings all day. But I'm free on Wednesday.*
Jeff Baker	*Then how about in the morning, say ten thirty?*
Pete Smith	*Wednesday at ten thirty? Just a moment. Yes, that would be fine.*

1 Why do they want to meet?

_____

2 Which day is best for Jeff?

_____

3 Why can't Pete meet then?

_____

4 When do they arrange to meet?

_____

2 Complete the schedule for Pete Smith.

Monday	9:15 Staff development meeting 12:00 Lunch with Hiroshi Saito
Tuesday	9:00–2:00 Sales meeting (regional reps) 3:15–4:15 HR meeting with Shelly
Wednesday	

1 Read the e-mail.

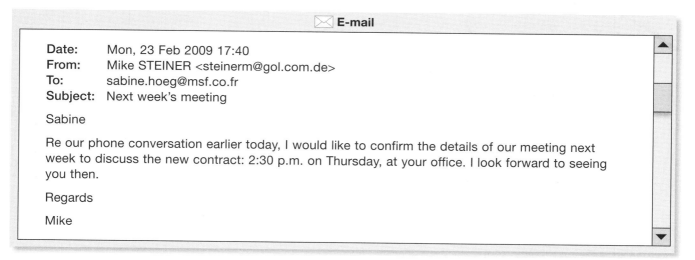

> ✉ **E-mail**
>
> **Date:**   Mon, 23 Feb 2009 17:40
> **From:**   Mike STEINER <steinerm@gol.com.de>
> **To:**   sabine.hoeg@msf.co.fr
> **Subject:** Next week's meeting
>
> Sabine
>
> Re our phone conversation earlier today, I would like to confirm the details of our meeting next week to discuss the new contract: 2:30 p.m. on Thursday, at your office. I look forward to seeing you then.
>
> Regards
>
> Mike

['Re' is short for 'regarding' and is commonly used in informal correspondence.]

2 Answer the questions. Use short answers.

Example
When was the e-mail sent?
5:40 p.m., Monday February 23rd, 2009

a Who wrote it?

_____

b Who is it to?

_____

c What is it about?

_____

d When did Mike phone Sabine?

_____

e When is the meeting?

_____

f Where is it?

_____

g What is the subject of the meeting?

_____

3 Look at the situation in Module 5.3, exercise 2. In the space below, complete a similar e-mail from Paula Kellerman to Eiji Takahashi.

✉ **E-mail**

Date: Tue, 30 June 2009 10:20
From: Paula KELLERMAN <kellermanp@mol.co.hu>
To: etakahashi@gol.com
Subject: _____

6

Requests and offers

MODULE 6.1

Placing an order

1 Number the lines of the telephone conversation in the correct order.

A *By August 20th? Certainly. So that's 500 GH600 LCD panels by August 20th.* ☐

B *Sure. It's Andersonb@gateway.com.* ☐

A *Hello. How can I help you?* ☐ 1

A *Certainly, Mr. Anderson. Which model would you like?* ☐

A *Yes, of course. Can I have your e-mail address, please?* ☐

A *500? Just one moment. Yes, no problem.* ☐

A *OK. And how many would you like?* ☐

B *500, please.* ☐

A *OK, I've got that. Goodbye, Mr. Anderson, and thank you.* ☐

B *Could you deliver them by August 20th?* ☐

B *It's Bill Anderson here. I'd like to order some LCD panels.* ☐ 2

B *Let's see, the order number is GH600.* ☐

B *Great. Could you send me confirmation by e-mail?* ☐

2 Put these jumbled requests in the correct order.

1 by   you   10th   Could   deliver   October   please   them   ?

_____

2 e-mail   Could   address   your   have   I   ?

_____

3 new   Could   me   please   your   send   catalogue   you   ?

_____

Requests and offers

1 Complete the requests. Use the words below.

install   mail   answer   e-mail

a Could you _____ these packages, please?

b Could you _____ the phone, please?

c Could you _____ this new software?

d Could you _____ him to cancel the meeting?

2 Complete the offers. Use the words below.

copy   open   call   order

a Would you like me to _____ Mr. Lee?

b Would you like me to _____ these reports?

c Would you like me to _____ the window?

d Would you like me to _____ lunch?

3 Match the offers with the correct answer.

a Would you like me to meet him   1 No, thanks. I have one already.
   at the airport?   2 Yes, please. It's flight VS 3.
b Would you like to see the itinerary?   3 Yes. What time do we start?
c Would you like me to send you
   our catalogue?

4 Write the questions. Use the prompts.

Example
could / send / new catalogue?
Could you send me your new catalogue, please?

1 could / send / price list / today?

   _____

2 could / scan / pages / for me?

   _____

3 could / meet Mr. Eve / airport / tomorrow?

   _____

4 could / visit / head office / Tuesday?

   _____

1 Match the words to the correct figure.

0.95	one point five
9.5	zero point seven five
0.75	zero point nine five
75.2	nine point five
1.5	zero point one five
0.15	seventy five point two

2 Look at the information. Answer the questions.

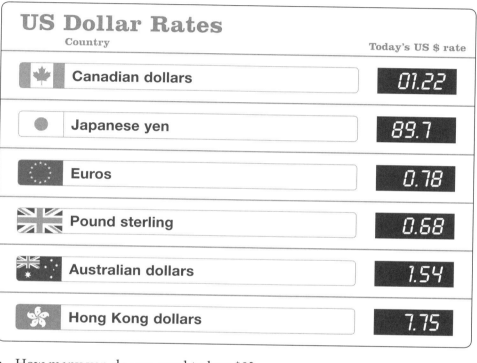

US Dollar Rates	
Country	Today's US $ rate
Canadian dollars	01.22
Japanese yen	89.7
Euros	0.78
Pound sterling	0.68
Australian dollars	1.54
Hong Kong dollars	7.75

a How many yen do you need to buy $2?

_____

b How much is $10 worth in GB pounds?

_____

c Which three countries have dollars as their currency?

_____

d What is the currency of Europe?

_____

3 Match the currency with the country.

Chinese   Japanese   Korean   Malaysian   Thai   Swiss

_____	yuan	_____	yen
_____	franc	_____	baht
_____	ringgit	_____	won

1   Match the e-mail and web address symbols with the words.

@	forward slash
s_p	hyphen
.	backslash
/	underscore
\	at
p-m	dot

2   What is the correct way to say the e-mail address below? Check (✓) the correct box.

My e-mail address is smith_p@apple.com

smith hyphen p dot apple dot com   ☐

smith underscore p at apple dot com   ☐

3   Does your company have a website? Write the address.

_____

4   Read the e-mail. Answer the questions.

✉ **E-mail**

Date: Thursday 05 September 2009 9:20
From: Paul Cooper [cooperp@yahoo.hk]
To: Cassandra Green
Subject: Arrival time

Thanks for your message. I'll be arriving at the station at 2:30 p.m. I look forward to meeting you then.

Best wishes,
Paul

a   Who is the message from?

_____

b   Who is it to?

_____

c   What is Paul's e-mail address?

_____

d   When did he send the message?

_____

e   What time will he arrive at the station?

_____

MODULE 6.5

1 Chae-Hyeon Park is ordering some printer cartridges for the office. Write the missing questions.

A *Good morning. This is PaperDirect. How can I help you?*
B *I'd like to order some printer cartridges, please.*
A *Certainly, ma'am. How many* _____ ¹?
B *We need 12, please.*
A *No problem. Which* _____ ²?
B *It's a Laserjet 1100.*
A *That's fine. What* _____ ³?
B *Black, please.*
A *Can* _____ ⁴?
B *Yes, my name is Chae-Hyeon Park and the address is BV Office, 250 W 38th Street, New York 10001.*
A _____ ⁵?
B *It's chpark@bv.op.com.*
A *OK. That comes to $722.78 including delivery. They'll be with you by lunchtime tomorrow.*
B *Thanks for your help.*

2 Match the names of the household appliances with the pictures.

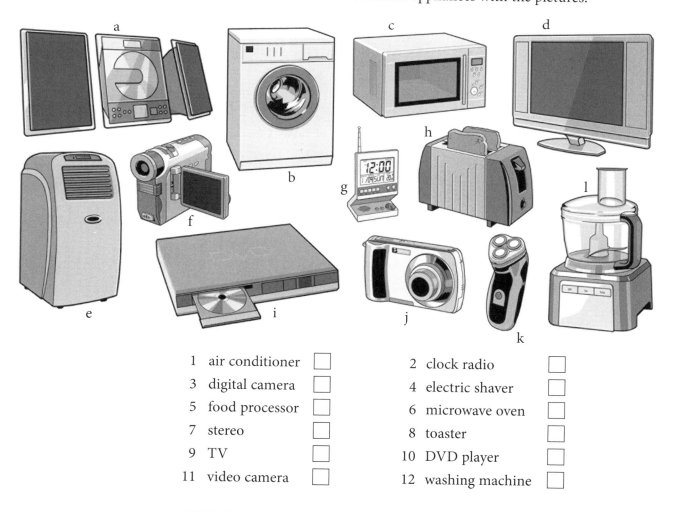

1	air conditioner ☐	2	clock radio ☐
3	digital camera ☐	4	electric shaver ☐
5	food processor ☐	6	microwave oven ☐
7	stereo ☐	8	toaster ☐
9	TV ☐	10	DVD player ☐
11	video camera ☐	12	washing machine ☐

1   Read this newspaper article about computers in the home.

Few people today realize how much we depend on computers in our daily lives. Most people have at least one computer at home; many families have more than one, if you include laptops as well. However, these are not the only computers found in the typical home.

A number of electronic devices, including washing machines and digital cameras, are controlled by powerful microprocessors. Electric shavers contain a microprocessor to charge the battery, and food processors have one to adjust the motor. Modern central heating and air-conditioning systems also use microprocessors to control the temperature in a house and save energy. Most of the computing power is used to make the device simple to use. Televisions and stereo systems usually contain the most powerful computing devices in the home. They are used for tuning, remote control, and speed control.

David Fanshawe, a development engineer with Philips, thinks that more and more computer-controlled products will appear in the near future. 'I don't think there are any computer-controlled toasters on the market yet, but I'm sure it will happen,' he says.

2   Are these sentences true or false? Check (✓) the correct box.

		True	False
a	Most people in developed countries have a lot of computers in their homes.	☐	☐
b	Batteries control the microprocessor.	☐	☐
c	Food processors generally contain the most powerful microprocessors.	☐	☐
d	David Fanshawe has developed a computer-controlled toaster.	☐	☐
e	Products controlled by microprocessors will be more common in the future.	☐	☐

7

Company and personal history

MODULE 7.1   Company history 1

1 Complete the sentences about Apple Inc. Put the words in brackets into the past tense.

a Apple Inc. (start up) _____ in April 1976, in California.

b In 1984, Apple (launch) _____ the Macintosh.

c In 1991, Apple (develop) _____ the PowerBook.

d In August 1998, Apple (introduce) _____ the iMac.

e In 2001, in Virginia and California, Apple (open) _____ the first Apple Stores.

f In the same year, Apple (put) _____ the iPod onto the market.

2 Read the information again. Answer the questions.

1 When did the company start up?

_____

2 Where did the company start up?

_____

3 Where did Apple open the first Apple Stores?

_____

4 When did Apple put the iPod on the market?

_____

3 Write about your company.

1 When did your company start up?

_____

2 Where did your company start up?

_____

3 What did your company do last year?

_____

MODULE 7.2

Company history 2

Put the information about Laura Ashley, the famous fabric designer, in the correct order.

a They opened their first factory in 1967 in Carno, Wales. ☐

b In 1998 MUI, a Malaysian company, bought a 40% share in Laura Ashley. ☐

c The company expanded in the 1970s, and opened more than 500 stores in 28 countries. ☐

d She sold her first home-printed design to a London department store. ☐

e After her marriage, Laura began printing fabrics at home. ☐ 2

f Laura Mountney was born in Wales in 1925. She married Bernard Ashley in 1949. ☐ 1

g After her death, the company had financial problems in the 1990s. ☐

h Now the company is expanding again. ☐

i The company continued to expand in the 1980s, but in 1985, Laura Ashley died after falling down the stairs. ☐

j The store soon wanted more designs, and sales were so good that the Ashleys decided to start their own business. ☐

1 Write questions about Laura Ashley.

Example

When *was Laura Ashley born*?

She was born in 1925.

a Where _____?

   She was born in Wales.

b When did _____?

   After her marriage.

c What did _____?

   Her first home-printed design.

d When _____?

   In 1967.

e How many _____?

   500.

f When _____?

   In 1998.

2 Answer these questions about yourself.

1 When were you born?

   _____

2 Where did you go to college?

   _____

3 What did you study?

   _____

4 What was your first job?

   _____

5 Where was it?

   _____

6 Who do you work for now?

   _____

1 Match the numbers.
       one thousand   1 000 000
       ten thousand   1 000
       one hundred thousand   100 000
       one million   10 000

2 Write the numbers in words.

       1500   _____

       15 000   _____

       150 000   _____

       1 500 000   _____

3 Look at the information about the most visited cities by international
       tourists in 2007. Answer the questions.

Estimated number of visitors in 2007	
City	**Millions**
London	15.34
Hong Kong	12.05
Bangkok	10.84
New York	7.65
Seoul	4.99
Shanghai	4.80
Kuala Lumpur	4.40

a   How many international tourists went to Bangkok in 2007?

    _____, 840,000.

b   Which cities had less than 5,000,000 visitors?

    Seoul, _____, Kuala Lumpur.

c   How many people visited Hong Kong?

    _____, 050,000.

d   Which city had twice as many visitors as New York? How many people
    visited?

    _____, 15,_____

4 Read the information and answer the questions.

In 2007, these tourist attractions in London were visited by a large number of visitors:

The British Museum	5 500 000 tourists
The Tower of London	2 000 000 tourists
St Paul's Cathedral	1 600 000 tourists

a What do you think are the most popular tourist attractions in your country? Write three:

_____

_____

_____

b Use the Internet. Find out how many visitors they had last year.

_____

_____

_____

MODULE 7.5   A family business

1 Look at this resumé.

1102 Eisenhower Avenue,
Newark, NJ 07911-2288

Tel: (201) 583-7262

Email: enajera@aol.com

Elizabeth Maria Najera

PROFESSIONAL EXPERIENCE

2008–Present   CNT TELEVISION NETWORK, New York, NY
Promotion Marketing Department, Marketing Assistant

2007–2008   HERRSCH COMMUNICATIONS, Milwaukee, WI
Marketing Assistant

EDUCATION

2003–2007   UNIVERSITY OF WISCONSIN – Parkside WI
Bachelor of Arts: Communications
Minors: Business Administration, French

SKILLS

Computers   Proficient user of Microsoft Word, Excel,
QuarkXPress, Adobe Photoshop

Languages   Spanish (bilingual), French (fluent), Japanese (basic)

REFERENCES ON REQUEST

---

2 Are these sentences about Elisabeth's resumé true or false? Check (✓) the correct box.

		True	False
a	Her name is at the top.	☐	☐
b	She includes her full mailing address.	☐	☐
c	Her phone number is below her e-mail address.	☐	☐
d	Her professional experience comes before her education.	☐	☐
e	She writes the most recent information first.	☐	☐
f	She includes her high school education.	☐	☐
g	She provides references with the resumé.	☐	☐
h	She doesn't mention her hobbies and interests.	☐	☐

3 Now answer the questions about Elizabeth. Circle *Yes* or *No*.

a	Did she study Business Administration?	Yes	No
b	Did she work for CNN?	Yes	No
c	Was she a marketing assistant in 2008?	Yes	No
d	Did she start work in New York in 2008?	Yes	No
e	Did she study at the University of Hawaii?	Yes	No

MODULE 7.6

Culture file – Job mobility

Look at the resume in Module 7.5. Use the page below to produce your own resumé.

Name:
_____

Contact details:
_____
_____
_____

PROFESSIONAL EXPERIENCE
_____ _____
_____ _____
_____ _____
_____ _____

EDUCATION
_____ _____
_____ _____
_____ _____

SKILLS
_____ _____
_____ _____
_____ _____

REFERENCES ON REQUEST

Making plans

MODULE 8.1 Announcing company plans

1 Ray and Sam are going to turn an old laundromat into a coffee shop. Match the objectives on the left with the plans on the right.

a encourage regular customers
b make the place relaxing
c project a quality image
d attract lunchtime customers
e attract businesspeople
f offer a friendly and efficient service

1 offer a wide range of sandwiches
2 install Wi-Fi
3 issue membership discount cards
4 train the staff well
5 play soft background music
6 serve the highest quality coffee

2 Ray and Sam need to borrow some money from the bank. They are talking to a loan officer about their plans. Use the ideas above to write five conversations.

Example

Ray	*We want to encourage regular customers.*
Loan officer	*How are you going to do that?*
Sam	*We're going to issue membership discount cards.*

a **Ray** _____

  Loan Officer _____ ?

  Sam _____

b **Ray** _____

  Loan Officer _____ ?

  Sam _____

c **Ray** _____

  Loan Officer _____ ?

  Sam _____

e **Ray** _____

  Loan Officer _____?

  Sam _____

f **Ray** _____

  Loan Officer _____?

  Sam _____

MODULE 8.2

Talking about company objectives

1 Look at this example.

open a new store / increase sales
A *Do you plan to open a new store?*
B *Yes. Our objective is to increase sales.*

Now write similar conversations.

a close some branches / reduce costs

  A _____?

  B _____

b hire more sales staff / increase our turnover

  A _____?

  B _____

c reduce your prices / increase our market share

  A _____?

  B _____

d use a new advertising agency / change our image

  A _____?

  B _____

2 Write about one of your company's objectives below. It can be real or imaginary.

Our objective is to

_____

_____

To do that, we're going to

_____

_____

We also plan to

_____

_____

MODULE 8.3   A business trip

1 Read the itinerary for Mr. Lucas's trip to Shanghai.

DATES		CITY AND ACTIVITIES
APRIL 30TH	AM	depart for Beijing
	PM	arrive Beijing
MAY 1ST	AM	meeting with Mr. Liu and office staff
	PM	visit hotel site
MAY 2ND		meet Dept of Commerce
MAY 3RD		depart for Shanghai
		arrive Shanghai
MAY 4TH	ALL DAY	Business Forum – the hotel group
MAY 5TH		sightseeing /shopping in Shanghai
MAY 6TH		depart China for USA

2 Complete the conversation between Mr Lucas and his colleague.

A *Can I check some dates with you? When are you out of the office?*
B *Next week. I'm visiting Beijing to meet Mr. Liu and the design team.*
A *Oh, that's right. When are you leaving?*
B *On _____[1]. I'm coming back on _____[2].*
A *OK. What are your plans in Beijing?*
B *I'm going to visit _____[3] on the 1st. And I have some meetings too.*
A *Who with?*
B *I'm meeting the _____[4] on the 2nd.*
A *Sounds interesting. Are you going to have any free time?*
B *Yes. I plan to go _____[5] in Shanghai on the final day.*
A *OK. Well, have a good trip!*

MODULE 8.4   Numbers – percentages

1 Match the numbers to the words.

1.4 %	one hundred and forty percent
14%	one point four percent
140%	fourteen percent

8.1%	eighty one percent
81%	zero point eight one percent
0.81%	eight point one percent

2 Match the numbers 1–11 in the chart with countries in a–h.

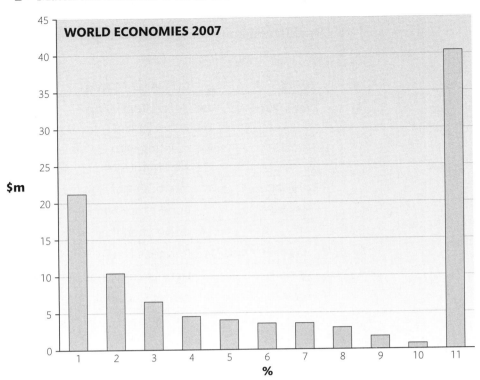

a The USA produces about 21.3% of the world's goods and services.
b The Rest of the World produces 40.5%.
c China produces 10.8% less than the USA.
d Japan produces 6.6%.
e India produces 2% less than Japan and 0.3% more than Germany.
f The UK produces 1% less than Germany.
g Russia produces 3.2%, 1% more than France.
h South Korea and Thailand have 1.8% and 0.8% of the total.

1 the USA   2 _____   3 _____   4 _____   5 Germany
6 _____   7 _____   8 _____   9 _____   10 _____
11 _____

3 Now write two sentences of your own about the information in the charts.

a _____
   _____
   _____

b _____
   _____
   _____

1 Sort the vocabulary into the correct category:

Hotel Facilities

taxi	gym	meeting rooms	shuttle bus
swimming pool	Wi-Fi	heliport	train link
business center	spa	video conferencing	tennis courts

Transportation	**Sports facilities**	**Conference facilities**
_____	_____	_____
_____	_____	_____
_____	_____	_____
_____	_____	_____

2 Look at the itinerary in Module 8.3. Mr. Price and Ms. Galloway are visiting your offices next month for three days. Write a similar schedule for their trip.

DATES	CITY AND ACTIVITIES

3 Now answer the questions. Use the information in the itinerary.
1 When are Mr. Price and Ms. Galloway going to arrive?
2 What are they going to do while they are here?
3 How long are they going to stay?
4 When are they leaving?

1 Read the memo from Paul Nardini, manager of the Sydney branch of IP Construction.

MEMO

To: Engineering Dept staff   **From:** Paul Nardini
Date: September 26   **Subject:** Sam Feinstein's visit

Sam Feinstein from the New York office plans to visit us in November. He is going to be here for one month, and plans to visit the Lagoon Hotel site. He wants to meet everyone on the engineering team.

Please give him any help you can.

---

2 Answer the questions. Use short answers.

a Who's the memo to?

_____

b Who's it from?

_____

c When was it written?

_____

d What's it about?

_____

3 Now write a similar memo. Use the words below. Write your own name and today's date.

Tom Chang   Taipei   April   three days
tour the new factory   discuss sales targets

MEMO

To: Sales Dept staff   **From:** _____
Date: _____   **Subject:** _____

_____

_____

_____

_____

_____

_____

9
Opinions and preferences

MODULE 9.1   Choosing the best candidate

1   AGM Foods wants to appoint an area sales manager for Asia. Read this information about the applicants.

Name:	Katie Chan
Experience:	4 years as sales representative, Empire Foods (Taipei)
Languages:	English, Chinese, Japanese
Qualifications:	BA in Business Studies MA Business Administration

Comments:

Confident. Has very clear objectives.

Asked very interesting questions.

Name:	Neil Unsworth
Experience:	8 years as sales representative, International Petroleum (Switzerland)
Languages:	English, French, German, elementary Japanese
Qualifications:	BSc in Mathematics MA in Economics

Comments:

Very confident, but no clear objectives.

Asked a few questions about salary and benefits.

2   Are these sentences true or false? Check (✓) the correct box.

		True	False
a	Unsworth has more work experience.	☐	☐
b	Chan speaks more Asian languages.	☐	☐
c	Unsworth has more experience in the food industry.	☐	☐
d	Chan has more qualifications.	☐	☐
e	Unsworth speaks more languages.	☐	☐
f	Chan has clearer objectives than Unsworth.	☐	☐
g	Unsworth seems to be more confident than Chan.	☐	☐
h	Unsworth asked more interesting questions.	☐	☐

3   Who would you employ?

MODULE 9.2

1 Complete the table.

Example

long   *longer*

1 slow   _____

2 cheap   _____

3 _____   more compact

4 noisy   _____

5 _____   more expensive

6 difficult   _____

7 complicated   _____

2 Read the conversation between a customer and a store clerk.

modem / expensive / cheap / slow

A *I'm looking for a modem.*
B *Certainly. How about this one?*
A *That's a little expensive. Do you have anything cheaper?*
B *This one is cheaper, but it's slower than the other one.*

Now write three similar converstions. Use the comparative forms of the words below.

a photocopier / large / small / expensive

A _____

B _____

A _____

B _____

b GPS / complicated to use / simple / less compact

A _____

B _____

A _____

B _____

c scanner / slow / fast / difficult to use

A _____

B _____

A _____

B _____

1   Read this survey of American diners. A diner is a restaurant which serves cheap, simple food. Customers often sit at the counter to eat.

	Diner	Food	Service	Décor	Cost
Chicago	Sam's Diner	★★★★	★★★	★★	$$$
Los Angeles	The Happy Dog Diner	★★★	★★★★	★	$$
Miami	Peggy Sue's Kitchen	★★	★★★	★★★★	$$$$
New Orleans	Oscar's Grill	★★★★★	★★★	★★★★	$$$$$

★ poor ➞ ★★★★★ excellent $ cheap ➞ $$$$$ expensive

2   Write six sentences comparing the diners for food, service, decor, or cost. Use these words to help you. Use a different word each time.

Example

The food at Oscar's Grill is better than the food at Peggy Sue's Kitchen.

food	good / nice / delicious	*The food at ...*
service	good / fast / slow	*The service at ...*
decor	good / attractive / nice	*The decor at ...*
cost	expensive / cheap	*The food at ...*

a _____

b _____

c _____

d _____

e _____

f _____

1 A customer is asking a store clerk about a new laptop. Complete the questions.

Example
How *high is it?*
It's 35 mm high.

1 How _____?
It's 280 mm deep.

2 How much _____?
It weighs 2.9 kg.

3 How much _____?
It has 4.5 GB of memory.

2 Look at these specifications. Answer the questions.

Example
Which model is heavier?
The Jpi is heavier.

	XJ 200	**Jpi 350**
Speed	1.75 Ghz	1.5 Ghz
Maximum memory	4.2 GB	4.3 GB
H x W x D	30 x 400 x 250	40 x 450 x 280
Weight	3 kg	4.1 kg
Cost	$$$	$$

a Which one is faster?

_____

b Which has more memory?

_____

c Which one is smaller?

_____

d Which one is more expensive?

_____

e Which one would *you* buy?

_____

MODULE 9.5 New offices

1 Read the information about Eagle House and the Wilde Building.

	Eagle House	**The Wilde Building**
Size	2000 square meters	3800 square meters
Location	City of London, central location in the capital	30 minutes to London by rail
Age	2 years	10 years
Transportation	Excellent transportation links with bus and underground stations nearby	Accessible from the freeway by car
Layout	Small individual offices	Open plan-offices, conference suites available, spacious interior
Facilities	Large reception area	Staff gym, canteen, parking

2 Write the questions and answers.

Example
(large) *Which office building is larger?*
The Wilde Building is larger.

1 (central) _____

2 (old) _____

3 (convenient) _____

4 (spacious) _____

5 (facilities) _____

3 Which office building would you choose?

MODULE 9.6 Business writing – a job application letter

1 A few months ago, Katie Chan saw this advertisement in a magazine.

AGM Foods

Far East Sales Manager

AGM Foods seeks a qualified, experienced person to head its Hong Kong sales office. Applicants should have previous sales experience, and speak at least one Asian language. Excellent salary and benefits.

Apply with resumé to Barry Devine, International Recruiting Manager, AGM Foods Inc., 4th Floor, Taikoo House, 979 Kings Road, Quarry Bay, Hong Kong.

This is her letter of application.

Dear Mr. Devine,

I am replying to your advertisement in the July 14th issue of Business Monthly, and enclose a copy of my resumé, as requested. I believe that I am suitably qualified for the position of Far East Sales Manager, as I have four years of experience in sales, and I speak Chinese and Japanese.

I look forward to hearing from you.

Sincerely,

Katie Chan

2 Write short answers to these questions.

a   What kind of job is being advertised?

_____

b   What kind of person do they want?

_____

c   What will the person do?

_____

d   What kind of experience should he / she have?

_____

e   How many Asian languages should he / she speak?

_____

f   What should he / she send?

_____

3 Now read this advertisement.

Economic News Reporter

Japan's leading economic newspaper seeks an Economic News Reporter, who will be based in London. Applicants should have previous journalistic experience and speak, read, and write English and Japanese. Excellent salary and benefits.

Apply with resumé to: **Mr. G Davidson, Economics Weekly,**
12 Cowper Court, London EC4.

4 Write an application for the position above. Use your own name and ideas. Use the letter in Exercise 2 to help you.

Directions and invitations

MODULE 10.1 | Finding your way

1 Look at this map. You are at the Wisma Atria Shopping Center. Read the directions below and write the destinations.

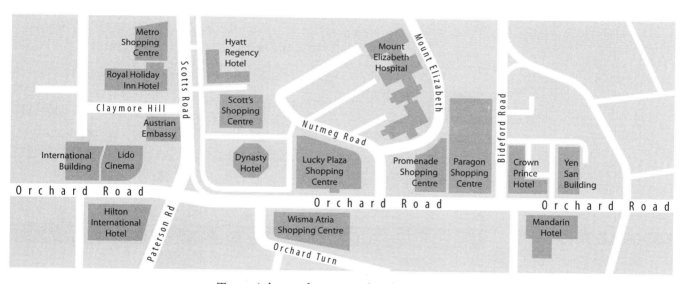

a Turn right, and go straight along Orchard Road.
It's on the left, just after the Promenade Shopping Center. _____

b Turn left, then turn right at the first intersection. Go straight along Scotts Road, and you'll see it on the left, across from the Hyatt Regency Hotel. _____

c Turn right, then take the first turn on the left. Turn right onto Mount Elizabeth. It's the large building on the left. _____

d Turn left, and go straight along Orchard Road. Go straight at the intersection. It's on the right, next to the Lido Cinema. _____

e Turn left, then turn right at the first intersection. Go straight along Scotts Road. It's the first large building on the left. _____

2 Now write two dialogues. A asks for directions from Scotts Shopping Center to two places on the map. B gives the directions.

A Excuse me, can you tell me how to get to _____?

B _____

A _____?

B _____

MODULE 10.2 Asking for and giving directions

Complete the directions. Use the words below.

Example
Go *straight* ahead.

next	across	between	left
on	past	second	~~straight~~

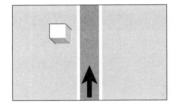

a It's on your _____.

b It's on your right, just _____ the hotel.

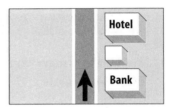

c It's _____ the bank and the hotel.

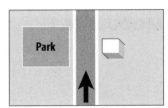

d It's _____ from the park.

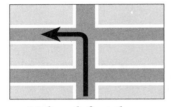

e Make a left at the _____ intersection.

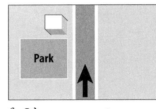

f It's _____ to the park.

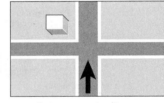

g It's _____ the corner.

MODULE 10.3 Apologies and invitations

1 Match the apologies (a–e) with the responses (1–5).
a I'm very sorry I'm late. I'm afraid I took a wrong turn.
b I'm sorry I can't show you the new model today. It's not ready yet.
c I'm sorry I don't have the exact figures right now.
d I'm really sorry I wasn't here to meet your flight, Mr. Kim. Have you been waiting long?
e I'm sorry I forgot to make your reservation.

1 Just a few minutes. Don't worry about it.
2 That's all right. The building is difficult to find.
3 Don't worry, but could you get them to me by tomorrow?
4 That's OK, but could you do it as soon as possible, please?
5 No problem. When do you think I can see it?

2 Now write an apology and a response. Use your own ideas.

A _____

_____

_____

B _____

_____

_____

3 Keiko Nakamura invites her colleague Lisa Neil to dinner. Put the lines of the conversation in the correct order.

B No, thank you. I'm sure I can find it. What time shall we meet? ☐

A Is 7:00 all right with you? We can meet at the restaurant. ☐

B Yes, I love it. ☐

B Thank you, Keiko. That would be very nice. ☐

A Would like to join me for dinner this evening, Lisa? 1

B Yes, 7:00 is fine. See you then. ☐

A Great. Do you like Chinese food? ☐

A OK. Let's go to the Shanghai Inn. It's just across from the station. Would you like me to draw you a map? ☐

MODULE 10.4   Numbers – travel times

Look at the tourist information for visitors to Hong Kong. Then answer the tourists' questions.

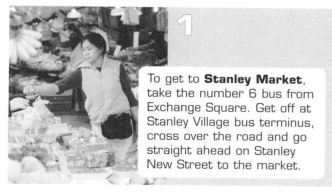

To get to **Stanley Market**, take the number 6 bus from Exchange Square. Get off at Stanley Village bus terminus, cross over the road and go straight ahead on Stanley New Street to the market.

To get to **Kam Shan Country Park**, take the number 81 bus going to Wo Che, from outside 777 Nathan Road.

The **Peak Tram** runs every day, at ten- to fifteen-minute intervals, starting at 7:00 a.m. The last journey is at 12:00 midnight.

To get to the **Jade Market**, take the MTR (Mass Transit Railway) to Yau Ma Tei and leave from Exit C.

1   Which bus goes to Stanley Market?

_____

2   Where should I get off the bus for Stanley Market?

_____

3   Which bus goes to Kam Shan Country Park?

_____

4   Where should I take the bus from to get to the Park?

_____

5   What time is the first Peak Tram?

_____

6   How often do the trams run?

_____

7   What time does the Peak Tram stop running?

_____

8   Which exit do I need for the Jade Market?

_____

MODULE 10.5

How do I get there?

Complete the travel crossword puzzle.

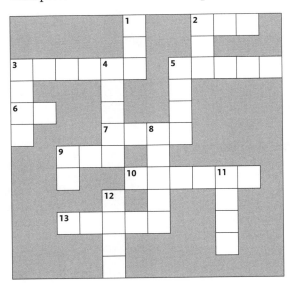

Across

2 It's started to rain. I'll call you a ___.
3 It was a twelve-hour ___. When we landed at Heathrow I was really tired.
5 I went to the wrong track and missed my ___.
6 My car broke down and I came the rest of the way ___ foot.
7 I think I'll take a cab. Is it a long ___ ?
9 I missed the last ___ and had to walk home.
10 It's a twenty–___ drive.
13 I always go to Paris by ___. It's only a short flight.

Down

1 How do I ___ to your office from the subway station?
2 I'll come by ___. I enjoy driving.
3 How long does it take on ___?
4 The flight takes about six ___.
5 How long does it ___ to get to the hotel from here?
8 It takes about one hour to ___ there, if the traffic isn't heavy.
9 It's quicker ___ bus.
11 I'm going on a business ___ to Seoul next month.
12 I often go to the park. It's just a short ___ from my apartment.

MODULE 10.6   Business writing – an invitation

1 Read the e-mail.

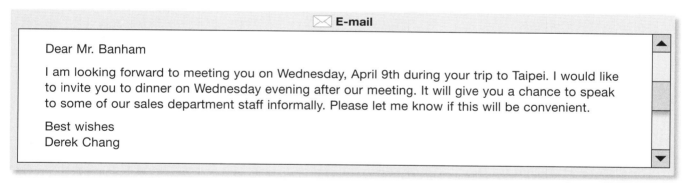

✉ **E-mail**

Dear Mr. Banham

I am looking forward to meeting you on Wednesday, April 9th during your trip to Taipei. I would like to invite you to dinner on Wednesday evening after our meeting. It will give you a chance to speak to some of our sales department staff informally. Please let me know if this will be convenient.

Best wishes
Derek Chang

2 Write a similar e-mail. Use your own name and this information.

Write to Lynn Kelly. She is going on a tour of your factory next week. Invite her to lunch before the tour. You want her to meet the export department staff informally.

11

Entertaining

MODULE 11.1

Offering food and drink

1 Put these jumbled sentences into the correct order.

a like   you   ?   appetizer   would   an

_____

b like   ?   would   drink   to   what   you

_____

c list   the   see   ?   you   would   like   wine   to

_____

d today's   what's   ?   soup

_____

e two   like   mineral   glasses   we'd   of   water

_____

2 Look at the sentences above. Who is speaking: the Server (S) or Customer (C)?

3 Put the conversation into the correct order.

Thank you. ☐

No, thanks. ☐

With milk? ☐

What would you like to drink? Tea or coffee? ☐

Here you are. ☐

I'd like a cup of coffee, please. ☐

1 Read this conversation. Then write some similar dialogues.

Example
a hamburger / a hot dog
A *Would you like something to eat? A hamburger or a hot dog?*
B *I'd like a hamburger, please.*
A *Here you are.*
B *Thank you.*

a a soft drink / some beer

A _____

B _____

A _____

B _____

b some steak / some fish

A _____

B _____

A _____

B _____

c a piece of cake / some ice cream

A _____

B _____

A _____

B _____

2 Find 15 items of food and drink in the word square.

H	W	I	N	E	M	I	L	K	O	I
G	A	D	E	S	S	E	R	T	R	E
I	T	X	Y	Z	W	R	Q	G	A	O
T	E	S	O	U	P	X	Y	A	N	G
L	R	T	O	M	A	T	O	R	G	F
I	V	E	G	E	T	A	B	L	E	N
O	O	A	D	W	G	Z	R	I	J	V
S	D	K	A	F	Y	G	E	C	U	I
E	K	R	L	I	Z	O	A	Z	I	L
A	A	Q	A	S	N	L	D	X	C	L
N	M	U	S	H	R	O	O	M	E	O

1 Look at the menu below. Then complete the conversation.

CATHY'S BISTRO

Lunch menu from 12:00 until 2:15

Two courses $28   Three courses $35

Appetizers

Soup of the day
Spring rolls
Salted soy beans
Green salad

Desserts

Chocolate fondue
Cheese and biscuits
Strawberry stack
Ice cream

Entrées

Steak
Lamb curry
Ramen noodles
Fried rice

Beverages

Cappuccino, latte
Tea, herbal teas
Cola, iced tea
Juice (orange, apple, grapefruit)

A *Are you ready to _____¹?*
B *Yes, I think so.*
A *_____² would you like to start?*
B *I'd _____³ the soup, please.*
A *Certainly. And _____⁴ your entrée?*
B *Can I _____⁵ the lamb curry, please?*
A *Yes, of course. _____⁶ you like something to drink?*
B *Yes, can I _____⁷ the wine list, please?*
A *Yes. _____⁸ you are.*

2 Decide what you would like to eat from the menu. Write a similar conversation.

A _____
B _____
A _____
B _____
A _____
B _____
A _____
B _____
A _____

1 Match the prices to the words.

$2.99	twenty nine dollars, twenty cents
$29.20	two hundred and twenty nine dollars
$229.00	two dollars ninety nine

2 Write the prices.

$7.50 _____

$75.00 _____

$ 750.00 _____

3 Unscramble these words. Then write the correct word in the questions below.

crrencuy _____   tosc _____

yap _____   refa _____

hechk _____

a What is the _____ of Japan? Is it the yen?

b How much was the taxi _____?

c I'd like to _____, please.

d May we have the _____, please?

e How much does it _____?

4 Write each price in two ways.

Example
$25.95   *twenty-five dollars and ninety-five cents*
          twenty-five ninety-five

a $63.44 _____

_____

b $8.70 _____

_____

c $99.99 _____

_____

d $9.06 _____

_____

e $70.18 _____

_____

f $88.80 _____

_____

5 Look at Ms. McKeith's expenses from a business trip last month. Answer the questions.

Airport shuttle bus	$35.00
Taxi fares	$22.00
Aug 2nd dinner	$76.20
Aug 3rd dinner	$41.64
Magazines	$12.50
Sightseeing	$61.75

a How much did she spend on transport?

_____

b How much did she spend on meals?

_____

c How much did she spend on sightseeing?

_____

MODULE 11.5   Ordering food and drink

1 Who says what? Label S (server) or C (customer).

Can I see the wine list, please?   _____

Please come this way.   _____

May I take your coat?   _____

Would you like something to drink?   _____

How was your meal?   _____

That was lovely, thank you.   _____

Are you ready to order?   _____

Can we have the check, please?   _____

How would you like to pay?   _____

2 Match the sentences (a–e) with the correct responses (1–5).
  a Can we have the check, please?
  b A table for two, please.
  c Can I take your coat?
  d Can we have some water, please?
  e Would you like to see the dessert menu?

  1 No, thanks. But could I have a coffee, please?
  2 Do you have a reservation?
  3 Yes, of course. Would you like mineral water?
  4 Certainly. How would you like to pay?
  5 Thank you. Here you are.

  a _____   b _____   c _____   d _____   e _____

1 Derek Chang sent Robert Banham an e-mail inviting him to dinner (see Module 10.6). Read the three possible e-mail replies to the invitation.

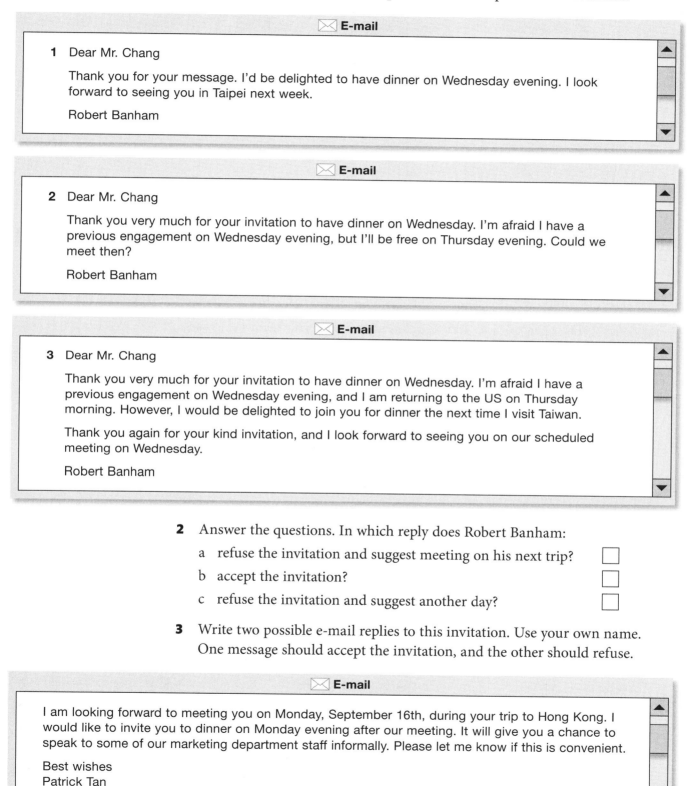

> ✉ **E-mail**
>
> **1** Dear Mr. Chang
>
> Thank you for your message. I'd be delighted to have dinner on Wednesday evening. I look forward to seeing you in Taipei next week.
>
> Robert Banham

> ✉ **E-mail**
>
> **2** Dear Mr. Chang
>
> Thank you very much for your invitation to have dinner on Wednesday. I'm afraid I have a previous engagement on Wednesday evening, but I'll be free on Thursday evening. Could we meet then?
>
> Robert Banham

> ✉ **E-mail**
>
> **3** Dear Mr. Chang
>
> Thank you very much for your invitation to have dinner on Wednesday. I'm afraid I have a previous engagement on Wednesday evening, and I am returning to the US on Thursday morning. However, I would be delighted to join you for dinner the next time I visit Taiwan.
>
> Thank you again for your kind invitation, and I look forward to seeing you on our scheduled meeting on Wednesday.
>
> Robert Banham

2 Answer the questions. In which reply does Robert Banham:

  a   refuse the invitation and suggest meeting on his next trip? ☐

  b   accept the invitation? ☐

  c   refuse the invitation and suggest another day? ☐

3 Write two possible e-mail replies to this invitation. Use your own name. One message should accept the invitation, and the other should refuse.

> ✉ **E-mail**
>
> I am looking forward to meeting you on Monday, September 16th, during your trip to Hong Kong. I would like to invite you to dinner on Monday evening after our meeting. It will give you a chance to speak to some of our marketing department staff informally. Please let me know if this is convenient.
>
> Best wishes
> Patrick Tan

12

Saying goodbye

MODULE 12.1

Saying goodbye

1 Complete the phrases. Use the words below.

forward   help   mention   pleasure   safe

a I look _____ to seeing you again next year.

b It was a _____ to meet you.

c Thank you for all your _____.

d Have a _____ trip home.

e Don't _____ it.

2 Match these phrases with the best replies.

a Goodbye. Have a good flight home.

b Please send my best wishes to the sales reps in Japan.

c It was a pleasure to meet you.

d I hope we'll meet again at the expo in Singapore.

1 Yes, so do I.

2 Thank you.

3 Yes, I will.

4 You, too.

1 Ms. Wade is saying goodbye to Mr. Ishii after a business trip to Kumamoto. Number the sentences in the conversation in the correct order.

A *Not at all. I hope we can meet again next year.* ☐

B *Then I'll be going. Well, goodbye, and thank you again.* ☐

B *I'm glad to hear it. And thank you for all your help.* ☐

A *That's good to hear. It's been useful for us, too.* ☐

A *I'd love to visit Canada. Oh, your taxi has just arrived.* ☐

A *It was a pleasure to meet you, Ms. Wade.* ☐ 1

B *Yes, I do, too. Perhaps next year we can meet in Toronto.* ☐

A *You're welcome. Goodbye, and have a safe journey.* ☐

B *I enjoyed meeting you, too, Mr. Ishii. It's been a useful visit.* ☐ 2

2 Look at the pictures. Complete the questions.

a Can I have your _____ address, please?
Yes, it's grady@whole-earth.aol.com.

b What's _____?
My cell number? Just a moment.
It's 07745 896 326.

c Do you have _____?
Yes. Here you are.

d What's your _____?
The office? It's 120 W 42 Street, New York, 10001. We're on the 28th floor.

1   Match the cues in the boxes with the expressions below.

a Thank your business acquaintance for his hospitality. 4 → **b** Respond politely. → **c** Give your business acquaintance a gift.

d Accept the gift. Ask if you can open it. → **e** Respond politely. → **f** Open the gift and thank student A.

1   Not at all. It's been a pleasure.
2   Oh, a fountain pen. Thank you very much.
3   Of course, go ahead.
4   Well, thanks for everything, Jack.
5   I hope you'll accept this small gift as a token of my appreciation.
6   Thanks, Harumi, that's very kind of you. Can I open it now?

2   Think about your future plans. Answer the questions.

Example
What are your plans for this week?
I'm meeting a new client on Monday.

1   What are your plans for next week?
    I'm _____
2   What are your plans for next month?
    I'm going to _____
3   What are your plans for next year?
    I'm not sure, but I think I'm going to _____
4   What are your plans for right now?
    I think I'll _____

1　Match the clocks with the times.

1 ☐ 　　2 ☐ 　　3 ☐

4 ☐ 　　5 ☐

a six thirty

b eleven p.m.

c ten p.m.

d five ten

e seven fifteen

2　Complete the chart.

seven o'clock in the evening	7:00 p.m.	1900
quarter after eleven at night	_____	2315
half past two in the afternoon	_____	_____
_____	_____	2245
twenty to seven in the evening	_____	_____
_____	10:20 p.m.	

3　Look at the train timetable from Tokyo to Gifu. Answer the questions.

■ TOKYO ► GIFU	
Tokyo	1803
Yokohama	1828
Shizuoka	2036
Toyohashi	2156
Nagoya	2247
Gifu	2309

a What time does the train leave Tokyo?

_____

b How many stops does it make before Gifu?

_____

c What time does the train leave Nagoya?

_____

d How long is the journey between Tokyo and Gifu?

_____

Itineraries

Look at the order of events at the MC Digital Media for Small Businesses Conference.

MCdigitalMedia

Saturday, March 15th

Time	Room 1	Room 2	Room 3
1000–noon	**Pre-conference workshops** Mike Lewis *Successful meetings*	Terry Vine *What is Digital Media?*	Janet Black *Small business forum*
1410–1530	Welcome and Announcements		
1530–1615	Keynote Speaker: Joe Watanabe [Prowse Software Solutions pty.]		
1630–1730	**Presentation 1** with Ann Cleaver	**Presentation 2** with Martin Han	**Presentation 3** with Julie Cheung
1800–1930	Opening Reception		
1930–	Free evening		

Answer the questions. Write short answers.

a   What time does the conference begin?

_____

b   Who is the keynote speaker?

_____

c   What time is he speaking?

_____

d   What time is Mr Han's presentation?

_____

e   How long does the opening reception last?

_____

1 Read this e-mail from Robert Banham.

✉ **E-mail**

To: Derek Chang
From: Robert Banham
Subject: My trip to Taipei

Dear Derek

Thank you very much for your hospitality during my trip to Taipei. Our meetings were very useful.

I particularly enjoyed the visit to the National History Museum in Taipei, and the meal at the Mongolian restaurant in the evening was wonderful. I look forward to returning the hospitality when you visit San Diego next year.

Thank you again.

Best wishes
Robert Banham

---

2 Write a similar e-mail. Use your own name and this information.

Write to Heidi Kleber about your trip to Germany last week. Use today's date. Your meetings were very productive. You visited the cathedral in Cologne and went to a Thai restaurant in the evening. The meal was delicious. Ms Kleber is going to visit you in your city next month.

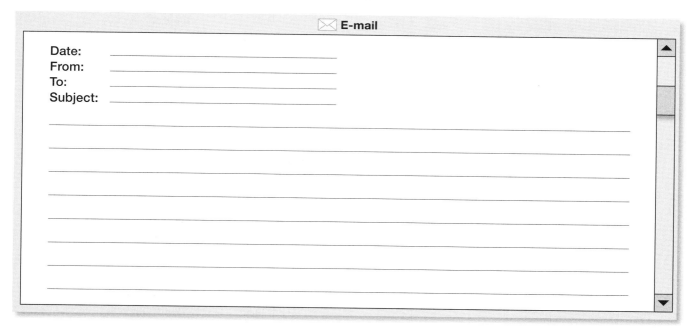

✉ **E-mail**

Date: _____
From: _____
To: _____
Subject: _____

Answer key

1 First meetings

MODULE 1.1
1 Pleased   2 meet
3 Welcome   4 trip
5 This   6 start

MODULE 1.2
1
  a He's from Seoul.
  b She works for Apple.
  c She lives in New York.
  d He's a marketing manager.
  e Where's Ms Cheng from?
  f Who does Mr Han work for?
  g Where does Mr Abe live?
  h What does Ms Griffin do?

MODULE 1.3
1
  a Flight VS 201
  b At 0815
  c Flight CX 251
  d Gate 17
2
  a What's the number for Narita Airport?
  b What's the number for Japan Railways?
  c What's your cell (phone) number?

MODULE 1.4
2
  a Studio Software Design has offices in Taipei.
  b Miho Ishida is an accountant.
  c Mark Wilson works in the Sales Department.
  d Bryce Anderson has branches in Tokyo, Seoul, London, Singapore, and Hong Kong.
  e Dr. Wu is a teacher of engineering.
  f Yoshiro Takeo's office is on the twelfth floor.
  g Kangnam International is a book company.
  h Michael Tseng is a software designer.

MODULE 1.5
a Tokyo   b works
c telephone   d Hong Kong
e address   f e-mail
g extension

MODULE 1.6
arrived, met, exchanged, shook, went, bowed

2 You and your company

MODULE 2.1
1
1 Pleased   2 for
3 with   4 in
5 department   6 do
7 organize
2
  a He works for IBM.
  b It sells computer hardware and software.
  c He works at the head Office.
  d She works for Samsung.
  e It makes consumer electronics.
  f She's a training manager.

MODULE 2.2
1
  a Toyota is a Japanese company. It makes cars.
  b China Mobile is a Chinese company. It provides telecom services.
  c Kraft is an American company. It sells food products.
  d Ricoh is a Japanese company. It makes electronic business products.
  e National Australia Bank is an Australian company. It provides banking services.
  f KFC is an American company. It sells fast food.

MODULE 2.3
1
2 designer   3 develop   4 manager
5 organize   6 supplier
2
1 I'm a website manager. I work in the IT department. I manage the company website.
2 I'm a training manager. I work in the Human Resources department. I organize staff training.
3 I'm a sales representative. I work in the Sales department. I demonstrate new products.
4 I'm an office clerk. I work in the Customer Service department. I check customer orders.

MODULE 2.4
1
12 twelve	16 sixteen
20 twenty	60 sixty
13 thirteen	17 seventeen
30 thirty	70 seventy
14 fourteen	18 eighteen
40 forty	80 eighty
15 fifteen	19 nineteen
50 fifty	90 ninety

2
  a How many factories does Sony have?
  b How many cars does Hyundai produce?
  c How many restaurants does Jollibee have?
  d How many ships does the Evergreen Marine Corporation have?

MODULE 2.5
1 name's   2 work   3 for
4 department   5 do

MODULE 2.6

1
a George Lorenzo
b Ms. Grace Wu
c George Lorenzo's visit to Beijing / his flight arrival time
d CA 452
e 2:30 p.m. (November 4th)

2 (Example answer)
Dear Ms. Wu,
Thank you for your e-mail of _____ , and your offer to meet me at the airport. My flight number is JL 765. That's Japan Airlines. It arrives at 6:00 p.m. on December 12th. I look forward to meeting you then.
Sincerely,
[your name]

3 Visiting a client

MODULE 3.1

1
a How   b take   c you
d This   e meet

2
1 Come in, Mr. Lewis. It's very nice to see you again. How are you?
2 I'm fine, thanks.
3 Oh, I'd like you to meet our marketing manager. This is Kenji Ito.
4 Hello, Mr. Ito. It's good to meet you.
5 Good to meet you, too, Mr Lewis.
6 Please, take a seat. Would you like some coffee before we start?
7 Yes, thank you.

MODULE 3.2

a Good morning. I have an appointment with Mr. Kawasaki at 11:15. I'm Grace Ma from Ricoh.
b Good afternoon. I have an appointment with Ms. Held at 2:20. I'm Toshi Ikeda from Futura Computers.
c Good afternoon. I have an appointment with Ms. Lee at 3:00. I'm Richard Bolton from Asia Week magazine.
d Good afternoon. I have an appointment with Mr. Allen at 3.30. I'm [your name] from [your company].

MODULE 3.3

Formal
A Good morning, Mr. Park.
B Good morning, Ms. Green. How are you?
A I'm very well, thank you.
B Please have a seat. Would you like a cup of coffee?
A Thank you. Coffee would be nice.

Informal
A Hey, Pon-chan.
B Hi, Jake. How's it going?
A Not so bad. How are your folks?
B Pretty good, thanks.
A Have a seat. Tea? Coffee?
B Coffee, please. Thanks!

MODULE 3.4

a next to   b across from
c down   d between

MODULE 3.5

1
100	one hundred
1000	one thousand
10 000	ten thousand
120	one hundred twenty
1200	one thousand two hundred
12000	twelve thousand

2
a two hundred (and) fifty
b three thousand
c nine hundred (and) seventy
d one hundred (and) eighty

4
c the address of the person you are writing to (the addressee)
a the return address (writer's address)
b the mailing information

5 1 e   2 g   3 c   4 a   5 h   6 b   7 d   8 f

6 a 3   b 1   c 4   d 2

7

Banner Creative Arts
463 Whitebrook Drive West
San Francisco
CA 94110
USA

Mr. H Leclerc
Personnel Director
Accents SA
18 Rue de Tocqueville
75430 Paris
France

DO NOT BEND

Banner Creative Arts
463 Whitebrook Drive West
San Francisco
CA 94110
USA

Mr. Jordi Pros
Marketing Manager
Fotosina S.A.
Fortuna Building
4th Floor, 21 Calle Roig
08005 Barcelona
Spain

URGENT

MODULE 3.6

2 a T   b F   c T   d T   e F   f F   g T   h T

4 Business activities

MODULE 4.1

1 a 5   b 1   c 4   d 6   e 3   f 2

MODULE 4.2

2
a He never mixes his job with his private life.
b He is always thinking about his family, not work.
c 'Never be satisfied' and 'Always question things'.
d He often has an idea when he's not happy with the way something works.
e They always think about how things can work better.
f No, they only occasionally give you the right answer.

MODULE 4.3

1
6 the customers buy the product
3 introduce the new flavors
1 do market research
4 organize advertising campaigns
2 run trial tests for the flavors
5 get product endorsement

2 Students' own answers

MODULE 4.4

1
1. 10:15
2. 11:20
3. 12:30
4. 1:45
5. 7:50

2
1. five to four
2. ten past four (ten after four)
3. a quarter after five
4. half past six
5. a quarter to nine
6. nine o'clock

3
a. Flight AC 869
b. It's at 10:08 a.m.
c. It flies to Dusseldorf.
d. It's at 11:10 a.m.
e. It's at 11:18 a.m.

MODULE 4.5

1
| 1 d, k | 2 a, c | 3 i, l |
| 4 b, f | 5 g, j | 6 e, h |

2 (Example answers)
Ted Finlay occasionally does work for Time magazine. He always works in his studio at home.
Anna Babic works for a shoe store chain. She manages the Fifth Avenue branch.
Derek Chan sells office equipment. He sometimes travels long distances to visit customers.
Ayako Yamamoto usually plays golf in the United States. Sometimes she appears in TV commercials.
Jack Givens works for a large construction company. He sometimes designs new office buildings.

MODULE 4.6

2 (Example answer)
Dear Ms. Wang
Thank you for your e-mail about the market research figures. 10:00 a.m. on Wednesday, November 12th at my office is fine. I look forward to seeing you then.
Best wishes
[your name]

5 Fixing an appointment

MODULE 5.1

1
a. What's she doing on Monday at 10:30?
b. What's she doing on Tuesday morning?
c. Is she meeting Marc Alder at 11:30?
d. When's she meeting Miho Harada?

2 Students' own answers

MODULE 5.2

1
| 1 morning | 2 could | 3 One |
| 4 speaking | 5 This | 6 do |

MODULE 5.3

1
B How about here on Thursday morning at 11:00?	6
B Hello, Julia, it's Akira Sato here.	2
A Great. I'll see you then. Bye.	9
A Next week would be fine. When do you have in mind?	5
A Julia Weber speaking.	1
B Bye.	10
B 2:00 p.m. on Thursday would be fine.	8
A Hi, Akira. What can I do for you?	3
B Could we meet next week to discuss the budgets?	4
A I'm sorry, but I'm busy all morning. But how about the afternoon, say 2:00 p.m.?	7

2 Students' own answers.

MODULE 5.4

1
January	1st	July	7th
August	8th	September	9th
October	10th	June	6th
May	5th	November	11th
December	12th	April	4th
February	2nd	March	3rd

2
a. March tenth, nineteen eighty four
b. May fifteenth, two thousand and one
c. July twenty-eighth, two thousand and eight
d. September thirtieth, two thousand and four
e. November first, two thousand and ten

MODULE 5.5

1
1. To discuss the new project.
2. Tuesday.
3. He has meetings all day.
4. Wednesday at 10:30.

2

Monday	9:15 Staff development meeting
	12:00 Lunch with Hiroshi Saito
Tuesday	9:00–2:00 Sales meeting (regional reps)
	3:15–4:15 HR meeting with Shelly
Wednesday	10:30 Meeting with Pete Smith

MODULE 5.6

2 a Mike Steiner
     b Sabine Hoeg
     c confirming the details of a meeting
     d earlier today
     e 2:30 p.m. on Thursday next week
     f at Sabine Hoeg's office
     g the new contract

3 Date   06.30.09.
     From   Paula Kellerman
     To   Eiji Takahashi
     Subject   This week's meeting
     Eiji
     Re our phone conversation earlier today, I would like to confirm the details of our meeting this week to discuss sales targets: 10:30 a.m. on Friday, at your office.
     I look forward to seeing you then.
     Regards
     Paula

6 Requests and offers

MODULE 6.1

1 **A** Hello. How can I help you?
     B It's Bill Anderson here. I'd like to order some LCD panels.
     A Certainly, Mr. Anderson. Which model would you like?
     B Let's see, the order number is GH600.
     A OK. And how many would you like?
     B 500, please.
     A 500? Just one moment. Yes, no problem.
     B Could you deliver them by August 20?
     A By August 20? Certainly. So that's 500 GH600 LCD panels by August 20th.
     B Great. Could you send me confirmation by e-mail?
     A Yes, of course. Can I have your e-mail address, please?
     B Sure. It's Andersonb@gateway.com.
     A OK, I've got that. Goodbye, Mr. Anderson, and thank you.

2 1 Could you deliver them by October 10th, please?
     2 Could I have your e-mail address?
     3 Could you send me your new catalogue, please?

MODULE 6.2

1 a Could you mail these packages, please?
     b Could you answer the phone, please?
     c Could you install this new software?
     d Could you e-mail him to cancel the meeting?

2 a Would you like me to call Mr. Lee?
     b Would you like me to copy these reports?
     c Would you like me to open the window?
     d Would you like me to order lunch?

3 a 2 b 3 c 1

4 1 Could you send me your price list today?
     2 Could you scan these pages for me?
     3 Could you meet Mr. Eve at the airport tomorrow?
     4 Could you visit head office on Tuesday?

MODULE 6.3

1 0.95   zero point nine five
     9.5   nine point five
     0.75   zero point seven five
     75.2   seventy five point two
     1.5   one point five
     0.15   zero point one five

2 a 179.4
     b £6.80
     c Canada, Australia, and Hong Kong
     d Euro

3 Chinese yuan   Japanese yen
     Swiss franc   Thai baht
     Malaysian ringgit Korean won

MODULE 6.4

1 @   at
     s_p   underscore
     .   dot
     /   forward slash
     \   backslash
     p-m   hyphen

2 smith underscore p at apple dot com

4 a Paul Cooper
     b Cassandra Green
     c cooperp@yahoo.hk
     d On September 5th
     e At 2:30 p.m.

MODULE 6.5

1 1 How many do you want / need?
     2 Which model is it?
     3 What color do you want / need?
     4 Can I have your name and address, please?
     5 What's your e-mail address, please?

2 1 e 2 g 3 j 4 k 5 l 6 c 7 a
     8 h 9 d 10 i 11 f 12 b

MODULE 6.6

2 a T b F c F d F e T

7 Company and personal history

MODULE 7.1

1 a started up   b launched   c developed
    d introduced   e opened   f put

2 1 (It started up) in April 1976.
    2 (It started up) in California.
    3 (It opened the first Apple Stores) in Virginia and California.
    4 (It put the iPod on the market) in 2001.

MODULE 7.2

1 f Laura Mountney was born in Wales in 1925. She married Bernard Ashley, a businessman in 1949.

2 e After her marriage, Laura began printing fabrics at home.

3 d She sold her first home-printed design to a London department store.

4 j The store soon wanted more designs, and sales were so good that the Ashleys decided to start their own business.

5 a They opened their first factory in 1967 in Carno, Wales.

6 c The company expanded in the 1970s, and opened more than 500 stores in 28 countries.

7 i The company continued to expand in the 1980s, but in 1985, Laura Ashley died after falling down the stairs.

8 g After her death, the company had financial problems in the 1990s.

9 b In 1998, MUI, a Malaysian company, bought a 40% share in Laura Ashley.

10 h Now the company is expanding again.

MODULE 7.3

1 a Where was Laura Ashley born?
    b When did she begin printing fabrics at home?
    c What did she sell to a London department store?
    d When did they open their first factory?
    e How many stores did the company open in the 1970s?
    f When did MUI buy a 40% share in Laura Ashley?

MODULE 7.4

1
one thousand	1000
ten thousand	10 000
one hundred thousand	100 000
one million	1000 000

2
1500	one thousand five hundred (fifteen hundred)
15 000	fifteen thousand
150 000	one hundred (and) fifty thousand
1 500 000	one million, five hundred thousand

3 a 10,840,000
    b Seoul, Shanghai, Kula Lumpur
    c 12,050,000
    d London, 15,340,000

MODULE 7.5

2 a T b T c F d T e T f F g F h T

3 a Yes   b No   c Yes
    d Yes   e No

8 Making plans

MODULE 8.1

1 a 3 b 5 c 6 d 1 e 2 f 4

2 a **Ray** We want to make the place relaxing.
     Loan Officer How are you going to do that?
     Sam We're going to play soft background music.

    b **Ray** We want to project a quality image.
     Loan Officer How are you going to do that?
     Sam We're going to serve the highest quality coffee.

    c **Ray** We want to attract lunchtime customers.
     Loan Officer How are you going to do that?
     Sam We're going to offer a wide range of sandwiches.

    d **Ray** We want to attract businesspeople.
     Loan Officer How are you going to do that?
     Sam We're going to install Wi-Fi.

    e **Ray** We want to offer a friendly and efficient service.
     Loan Officer How are you going to do that?
     Sam We're going to train the staff well.

MODULE 8.2

1 a **A** Do you plan to close some branches?
     B Yes. Our objective is to reduce costs.

    b **A** Do you plan to hire more sales staff?
     B Yes. Our objective is to increase our turnover.

    c **A** Do you plan to reduce your prices?
     B Yes. Our objective is to increase our market share.

    d **A** Do you plan to use a new advertising agency?
     B Yes. Our objective is to change our image.

MODULE 8.3

1 April 30th
2 May 6th
3 Mr Lin / the hotel site
4 Department of Commerce
5 shopping and sightseeing

MODULE 8.4

1

1.4%	one point four percent
14%	fourteen percent
140%	one hundred and forty percent

8.1%	eight point one percent
81%	eighty one percent
0.81%	zero point eight one percent

2
1	the USA	2	China	3	Japan
4	India	5	Germany	6	the UK
7	Russia	8	France	9	South Korea
10	Thailand	11	The Rest of the World		

3 Students' own answers

MODULE 8.5

1

Transportation	Sports facilities	Conference facilities
taxi	gym	business center
train link	spa	meeting rooms
shuttle bus	swimming pool	video conferencing
heliport	tennis courts	Wi-Fi

MODULE 8.6

2
a Engineering Department staff
b Paul Nardini
c September 26th
d Sam Feinstein's visit

3 (Example answer)

To	Sales Department staff
From	[your name]
Date	[today's date]
Subject	Tom Chang's visit

Tom Chang from the Taipei office plans to visit us in April. He is going to be here for three days, and plans to tour the new factory. He wants to discuss sales targets.
Please give him any help you can.

9 Opinions and preferences

MODULE 9.1

2 a T b T c F d F e T f T g T h F

3 Students' own answer

MODULE 9.2

1
1 slower
2 cheaper
3 compact
4 noisier
5 expensive
6 more difficult
7 more complicated

2
a **A** I'm looking for a photocopier.
  B How about this one?
  A That's a little large. Do you have anything smaller?
  B This one is smaller, but it's more expensive than the other one.
b **A** I'm looking for a GPS.
  B How about this one?
  A That's a little complicated to use. Do you have anything simpler?
  B This one is simpler, but it's less compact than the other one.
c **A** I'm looking for a scanner.
  B How about this one?
  A That's a little slow. Do you have anything faster?
  B This one is faster, but it's more difficult to use than the other one.

MODULE 9.3

2 (Example answers)
a The service at The Happy Dog Diner is faster than the service at Sam's Diner.
b Sam's Diner is cheaper than Peggy Sue's Kitchen.
c The decor at Oscar's Grill is more attractive than the decor at The Happy Dog Diner.
d The food at Oscar's Grill is nicer than the food at Peggy Sue's kitchen.
e The decor at the Peggy Sue's Kitchen is better than the decor at Sam's Diner.
f Peggy Sue's Kitchen is more expensive than Sam's Diner.

MODULE 9.4

1
1 How deep is it?
2 How much does it weigh?
3 How much memory does it have?

2
a The XJ 200 is faster.
b The Jpi 350 has more memory.
c The XJ 200 is smaller.
d The XJ 200 is more expensive.
e Students' own choice

MODULE 9.5

2
1 Which office building is more central?
  Eagle House
2 Which office building is older?
  The Wilde Building
3 Which office building is more convenient?
  Eagle House
4 Which building is more spacious?
  The Wilde Building
5 Which building has more facilities?
  The Wilde Building

3 Students' own choice

MODULE 9.6

2
a Far East Sales Manager
b qualified, experienced
c head the Hong Kong sales office
d previous sales experience
e at least one
f a resumé

4 Students' own answers

10 Directions and invitations

MODULE 10.1

1
a Paragon Shopping Center
b Royal Holiday Inn Hotel
c Mount Elizabeth Hospital
d International Building
e Austrian Embassy

MODULE 10.2

a It's on your left.
b It's on your right, just past the hotel.
c It's between the bank and the hotel.
d It's across from the park.
e Make a left at the second intersection.
f It's next to the park.
g It's on the corner.

MODULE 10.3

1 a 2 b 5 c 3 d 1 e 4

2 Students' own answers

3
A Would you like to join me for dinner this evening, Lisa?
B Thank you, Keiko. That would be very nice.
A Great. Do you like Chinese food?
B Yes, I love it.
A OK. Let's go to the Shanghai Inn. It's just across from the station. Would you like me to draw you a map?
B No, thank you. I'm sure I can find it. What time shall we meet?
A Is 7:00 all right with you? We can meet at the restaurant.
B Yes, 7:00 is fine. See you then.

MODULE 10.4

1 The number 6 bus goes to Stanley Market.
2 You should get off at Stanley Village bus terminus.
3 The number 81 bus goes to Kam Shan Country Park.
4 You should take the bus from outside 777 Nathan Road.
5 The first Peak Tram is at 7:00 a.m.
6 The trams run every ten to fifteen minutes.
7 The Peak Tram stops running at midnight.
8 You need Exit C for the Jade Market.

MODULE 10.5

MODULE 10.6

2 (Example answer)
Dear Ms. Kelly
I am looking forward to meeting you next week when you come on a tour of our factory. I would like to invite you to lunch before the tour. It will give you a chance to meet the export department staff informally. Please let me know if this will be convenient.
Best wishes
[your name]

MODULE 11.1

1,2 a Would you like an appetizer? S
  b What would you like to drink? S
  c Would you like to see the wine list? S
  d What's today's soup? C
  e We'd like two glasses of mineral water. C

3 What would you like to drink? Tea or coffee?
  I'd like a cup of coffee, please.
  With milk?
  No, thanks.
  Here you are.
  Thank you.

MODULE 11.2

1 (Example answers)
  A Would you like something to drink? A soft drink or some beer?
  B I'd like a beer, please.
  A Here you are.
  B Thank you.

  A Would you like something to eat? Some steak or some fish?
  B I'd like some fish, please.
  A Here you are.
  B Thank you.

  A Would you like something to eat? A piece of cake or some ice cream?
  B I'd like some ice cream, please.
  A Here you are.
  B Thank you.

2

H	W	I	N	E	M	I	L	K	O	I
G	A	D	E	S	S	E	R	T	R	E
I	T	X	Y	Z	W	R	Q	G	A	O
T	E	S	O	U	P	X	Y	A	N	G
L	R	T	O	M	A	T	O	R	G	F
I	V	E	G	E	T	A	B	L	E	N
O	O	A	D	W	G	Z	R	I	J	V
S	D	K	A	F	Y	G	E	C	U	I
E	K	R	L	I	Z	O	A	Z	I	L
A	A	Q	A	S	N	L	D	X	C	L
N	M	U	S	H	R	O	O	M	E	O

MODULE 11.3

1 1 order   2 What   3 like
  4 for   5 have   6 Would
  7 see / have   8 Here / There

2 Students' own answers

MODULE 11.4

1 $2.99   two dollars ninety nine
  $29.20   twenty nine dollars, twenty cents
  $229.00   two hundred and twenty nine dollars

2 seven dollars fifty cents
  seventy five dollars
  seven hundred (and) fifty dollars

3 currency
  pay
  check
  cost
  fare

  a What is the currency of Japan? Is it the yen?
  b How much was the taxi fare?
  c I'd like to pay, please.
  d May we have the check, please?
  e How much does it cost?

4 a sixty-three dollars and forty-four cents
    sixty-three forty-four
  b eight dollars and seventy cents
    eight seventy
  c ninety-nine dollars and ninety-nine cents
    ninety-nine ninety-nine
  d nine dollars and six cents
    nine dollars six
  e seventy dollars and eighteen cents
    seventy eighteen
  f eighty-eight dollars and eighty cents
    eighty-eight eighty

5 a She spent $57 on transport.
  b She spent $117.84 on meals.
  c She spent $61.75 on sightseeing.

MODULE 11.5

1 Can I see the wine list, please? C
  Please come this way. S
  May I take your coat? S
  Would you like something to drink? S
  How was your meal? S
  That was lovely, thank you. C
  Are you ready to order? S
  Can we have the check, please? C
  How would you like to pay? S

2 a 4   b 2   c 5   d 3   e 1

MODULE 11.6

2 a 3   b 1   c 2

3 (Example answers)
Dear Mr. Tan
Thank you very much for your invitation. I'd be delighted to have dinner with you on Monday evening. I look forward to seeing you in Hong Kong next week.
[your name]

Dear Mr. Tan
Thank you very much for your invitation to have dinner with you on Monday. I'm afraid I have a previous engagement on Monday evening, and I am returning to [your country] on Tuesday morning. But I'd be delighted to join you for dinner the next time I visit Hong Kong.
Thank you again for your kind invitation, and I look forward to seeing you for our scheduled meeting next Monday.
[your name]

12 Saying goodbye

MODULE 12.1

1 a I look forward to seeing you again next year.
   b It was a pleasure to meet you.
   c Thank you for all your help.
   d Have a safe trip home.
   e Don't mention it.

2 a 2   b 3   c 4   d 1

MODULE 12.2

1 **A** It was a pleasure to meet you, Ms. Wade.
   B I enjoyed meeting you, too, Mr. Ishii. It's been a useful visit.
   A That's good to hear. It's been useful for us, too.
   B I'm glad to hear it. And thank you for all your help.
   A Not at all. I hope we can meet again next year.
   B Yes, I do, too. Perhaps next year we can meet in Toronto.
   A I'd love to visit Canada. Oh, your taxi has just arrived.
   B Then I'll be going. Well, goodbye, and thank you again.
   A You're welcome. Goodbye, and have a safe journey.

2 a Can I have your e-mail address please?
   b What's your cell (phone) number?
   c Do you have a business card?
   d What's your work address?

MODULE 12.3

1 a 4   b 1   c 5   d 6   e 3   f 2

MODULE 12.4

1 1 d   2 a   3 e   4 c   5 b

2
seven o'clock in the evening	7:00 p.m.	1900
quarter after eleven at night	11:15 p.m.	2315
half past two in the afternoon	2:30 p.m.	1430
quarter to eleven in the evening	10:45 p.m.	2245
twenty to seven in the evening	6:40 p.m.	1840
twenty past ten at night	10:20 p.m.	2220

3 a It leaves Tokyo at 1803.
   b Four.
   c It leaves Nagoya at 2247.
   d Five hours and six minutes.

MODULE 12.5

   a It begins at 10:00 a.m.
   b The keynote speaker is Joe Watanabe.
   c He is speaking at 1530.
   d Mr. Han's presentation is at 1630.
   e The opening reception lasts one and a half hours.

MODULE 12.6

2 (Example answer)
To   Heidi Kleber
From   [your name]
Subject   My trip to Germany
Date   [today's date]
Dear Heidi
Thank you very much for your hospitality during my trip to Germany. Our meetings were very productive.
I particularly enjoyed the visit to the cathedral in Cologne, and the meal at the Thai restaurant in the evening was delicious. I look forward to returning the hospitality when you visit [your city] next month.
Thank you again.
Best wishes
[your name]